Introducing Dickens

John Kassman

D1380305

Unwin Hyman

ACKNOWLEDGEMENTS

Thanks are due to Mike Renton, for his help with original design ideas, especially on pages 5–7. The author and publishers would also like to thank the following for permission to reproduce illustrations.

BBC Hulton Picture Library, p. 12 (above)
The British Library, by permission of, p. 13 (top left)
City of Manchester Galleries, p. 40
The Dickens House Museum, pp. 4, 5 (top left), 6 (centre left, bottom left), 9, 10, 12 (below), 13 (right), 15, 24, 26, 41, 57, 64, 92

Mander & Mitchenson Theatre Collection, p. 5 (bottom)
Mansell Collection, p. 37
Stills from the film *Great Expectations* by courtesy of The Rank Organisation plc, pp. 45, 48, 51, 52, 53
Weidenfeld & Nicholson Archives, pp. 5 (centre left), 6 (bottom right), 7 (top left, bottom left, bottom right, centre), 13 (bottom left), 21, 30, 33, 42, 56, 61, 63 (left), 65 (right), 66, 72, 80, 83, 94; and the British Library, p. 6 (centre); and the Dickens House Museum, pp. 5 (top right, centre), 7 (centre right, top right), 11, 19, 21, 55, 63, 70, 71; and the Trustees of the Science Museum, p. 38

Published by UNWIN HYMAN
15–17 Broadwick Street
London W1V 1FP

© John Kassman 1988

British Library Cataloguing in Publication Data

Kassman, John
  Introducing Dickens.
  1. Fiction in English. Dickens, Charles,
  1812–1870. For schools
  I. Title
  823'.8

ISBN 0 7135 2788 9

Designed by Geoffrey Wadsley
Cover illustration reproduced by permission of the Dickens House Museum
Typeset by Cambridge Photosetting Services
Printed in Great Britain

Contents

George Cruikshank

George Cruikshank

Introduction: What the Dickens!

Everybody knows something about Charles Dickens: Scrooge at Christmas, Oliver Twist in the workhouse, Fagin and the pickpockets. His novels have been turned into plays, musicals, films, television series, radio adaptations. They have been translated into many languages and his name is familiar everwhere. What do *you* know about him?

This book is intended as an introduction to his life and work. It will tell you about his life and times and introduce you to a wide range of his writing. It is intended to make you curious and to guide your reading towards some of the liveliest novels ever written.

NOTE TO TEACHERS

The starting point of this book is that Dickens is a great comic writer. Other aspects of his art and career are then explored once this most important point has been established. The book is intended to de-mythologize Dickens and to provide such biographical and historical information as increases the accessibility of the novels and of the extracts quoted. Above all, it is intended to give pupils practice at reading Dickens's prose so that their subsequent experiences as readers of the novels will be positive and enjoyable. Many of the questions posed at the end of the extracts are genuinely open ended and are suitable for both written and oral work. Pupils thinking of doing Dickens as an 'open study' for GCSE English Literature may find the 'Select bibliography' section particularly helpful.

Note: Page references, where given, are to the Penguin edition of the novels.

Elizabeth Dickens

Charles's parents

John Dickens

's a boy!! It's a boy!!!

The life of Charles Dickens

EDITORS BOX

Charles was born on Friday 7th February 1812 in Portsmouth. His father was a pay clerk in the Navy Pay Office.

While working as a Parliamentary Reporter Charles had a number of stories published. His first publication was *A Dinner at Poplar Walk* – 1st December 1833. He wrote under the pen-name of 'Boz'.

1824. The family was in financial difficulties. Living at 16 Bayham Street, Camden Town, London.
The young Charles was sent to work in a factory, pasting labels onto bottles of boot blacking. His weekly wage was six shillings (30p). After a few months he went back to school but remained very shaken by his experience of the factory.

● Charles left school aged 15 and went to work in a solicitor's office. He learnt shorthand in his spare time and became a free-lance Court Reporter. By 1831 he was working as a Parliamentary Reporter and soon had a high reputation for speed and accuracy. He continued to work as a reporter until 1836.

● 1836: *Sketches by Boz* was published. Dickens was then asked to write stories to accompany a set of drawings. This developed into his first novel, *The Pickwick Papers*, issued in parts over a number of months. Sales reached 40,000 per issue. 'Boz' was now a celebrity at the age of 24.

Fine achievement eh, Mr Pickwick?

● In 1836 he married Catherine Hogarth.

'Mr Pickwick approached Bill Sikes.'.. no, that's wrong, damnit!

● While he was finishing *Pickwick Papers* he started writing *Oliver Twist* which was also published in monthly parts.

'Oliver Nickleby was born in a poorhouse......' NO!!

● In April 1838 publication was started of *Nicholas Nickleby*. (Oliver T. was still being finished!)

● 1840. Charles (now a father of three) started his own weekly magazine: *Master Humphrey's Clock*. He used the magazine to publish his next two novels *The Old Curiosity Shop* and *Barnaby Rudge*.

PARA ITALY

C.D.

● In Autumn of 1842 he started *Martin Chuzzlewit*. Christmas 1843, while in the middle of hi[s] novel, he wrote and publishe[d] *A Christmas Carol*. In the summer of 1844 he left for Ital[y] with his wife, four children, th[ree] servants, sister-in-law and do[g]

● On the 4th January 1842 he sailed to America. He returned at the end of June – disappointed by America – particularly over the issue of slavery.

● In the summer of 1845 he returned from Italy. That Autumn he performed, as an amateur, in a play with his friends. Prince Albert attended a Charity Performance. In the winter of 1845/6 he worked briefly as a newspaper editor on a new paper the *Daily News*.

← *Dickens the actor*

● 9th June 1870. Charles Dickens died quite suddenly, in Gads Hill Place. He was buried in Westminster Abbey.

Mrs D.

Ellen C.D. Ternan

● In April 1858 Dickens separated from his wife. They had been married for 22 years. Dickens wrote and published a criticism of his wife – saying that she had been a bad mother! Mrs D. and her son Charles moved into a house provided for them in Regents Park. The other eight children remained in C.D.'s household under the care of Georgina – Catherine's sister. The couple separated over Dickens's involvement with Ellen Ternan, a young actress.

● In the summer of 1846 Dickens was now the father of six children. After a break from novel writing of two years he began writing *Dombey and Son* (finished 1848). He continued to work at a slower pace than in the early years:
  1849–50 . . . *David Copperfield*.
  1852–53 . . . *Bleak House*.
  1854 . . . *Hard Times*.
  1855–57 . . . *Little Dorrit*.
  1859 . . . *A Tale of Two Cities*.
  1860–61 . . . *Great Expectations*.
  1864–65 . . . *Our Mutual Friend*.
In 1870 he started *The Mystery of Edwin Drood* but died while it was still unfinished.

● From 1850 onwards Dickens worked as the editor of his own magazines:
1850–59 – *Household Words*
1859–70 – *All The Year Round*.

● In 1858 he gave his first Public Readings tour. He did several of these over the next twelve years. His most famous and profitable tour was to America – November 1867–April 1868.

1

The making of 'Boz'

Dickens first achieved fame using the pen-name 'Boz'. This was as a very young man, following an unusual childhood, a disrupted education and a love-lorn adolescence.

Dickens's father, John Dickens, was not really a very successful man: he always enjoyed a party but frequently ran out of money. When Charles was a boy his father had a good job as a clerk in the Navy. Consequently Charles's first few years were spent in naval towns: first Portsmouth and then Chatham. Dickens both loved and was infuriated by his father, who later used to rely on his famous son to help him out of financial scrapes. When Dickens created the character of Wilkins Micawber in *David Copperfield* he was clearly drawing on his father's charms and failings. Here is Mr Micawber giving some advice to young David Copperfield.

'**M**y dear young friend,' said Mr Micawber, 'I am older than you; a man of some experience in life, and – and of some experience, in short, in difficulties, generally speaking. At present, and until something turns up (which I am, I may say, hourly expecting), I have nothing to bestow but advice. Still my advice is so far worth taking, that – in short, that I have never taken it myself, and am the' – here Mr Micawber, who had been beaming and smiling, all over his head and face, up to the present moment, checked himself and frowned – 'the miserable wretch you behold.'

'My dear Micawber!' urged his wife.

'I say,' returned Mr Micawber, quite forgetting himself, and smiling again, 'the miserable wretch you behold. My advice is, never do tomorrow what you can do today. Procrastination is the thief of time. Collar him!'

'My poor papa's maxim,' Mrs Micawber observed.

* * *

'My other piece of advice, Copperfield,' said Mr Micawber, 'you know. Annual income twenty pounds, annual expenditure nineteen nineteen and six, result happiness. Annual income twenty pounds, annual expenditure twenty pounds ought and six, result misery. The blossom is blighted, the leaf is withered, the god of day goes down upon the dreary scene, and – and in short you are for ever floored. As I am!'

To make his example the more impressive, Mr Micawber drank a glass of punch with an air of great enjoyment and satisfaction, and whistled the College Hornpipe.

From *David Copperfield*, Ch. 12, pp. 230–31

(For more about Mr Micawber, see *David Copperfield*, Chapters 9 and 11.)

John Dickens, Charles's father

Elizabeth, Dickens's mother, must have led a life of constant worry; with a large family to raise – she had six children – she must have found her husband's financial failures very trying. Not that she was a financial wizard – one of her money-losing schemes was to set up a school for young ladies. She liked to think that she was from a 'better' family than her husband. Her father had held quite a senior post as an administrator in the Navy. However, he left his post in disgrace after he had been discovered stealing money from the Navy. He had to run away to the Continent to avoid imprisonment. This happened shortly after Elizabeth married John Dickens and the scandal must have been difficult for her to bear. She certainly became quite hard-hearted – at least her son Charles thought of her in this way. He also thought of her as being rather silly and when he created the character of Mrs Nickleby he used his mother as his model. He was amused that she failed to spot the resemblance. In the following extract we find Mrs Nickleby in a fluster on being introduced to Lord Frederick Verisopht, who then asks after her daughter.

'Upon my soul, it's a most delightful thing,' said Lord Frederick, pressing forward: 'How de do?'

Mrs Nickleby was too much flurried by these uncommonly kind salutations, and her regrets at not having on her other bonnet, to make any immediate reply, so she merely continued to bend and smile, and betray great agitation.

'A – and how is Miss Nickleby?' said Lord Frederick. 'Well, I hope?'

'She is quite well, I'm obliged to you, my lord,' returned Mrs Nickleby, recovering. 'Quite well. She wasn't well for some days after that day she dined here, and I can't help thinking, that she caught cold in that hackney coach coming home: Hackney coaches, my lord, are such nasty things, that it's almost better to walk at any time, for although I believe a hackney coachman can be transported for life, if he has a broken window, still they are so reckless, that they nearly all have broken windows. I once had a swelled face for six weeks, my lord, from riding in a hackney coach – I think it was a hackney coach,' said Mrs Nickleby reflecting, 'though I'm not quite certain, whether it wasn't a chariot; at all events I know it was a dark green, with a very long number, beginning with a nought and ending with a nine – no, beginning with a nine, and ending with a nought, that was it, and of course the stamp office people would know at once whether it was a coach or a chariot if any inquiries were made there – however that was, there it was with a broken window, and there was I for six weeks with a swelled face – I think that was the very same hackney coach, that we found out afterwards, had the top open all the time, and we should never even have known it, if they hadn't charged us a shilling an hour extra for having it open, which it seems is the law, or was then, and a most shameful law it appears to be – I don't understand the subject, but I should say the Corn Laws could be nothing to *that* act of Parliament.'

Having pretty well run herself out by this time, Mrs Nickleby stopped as suddenly as she had started off, and repeated that Kate was quite well. 'Indeed,' said Mrs Nickleby, 'I don't think she ever was better, since she had the hooping-cough, scarlet-fever and measles, all at the same time, and that's the fact.'

From *Nicholas Nickleby*, Ch. 26, pp. 414–15

(See Chapters 21, 41 and 49 for some further examples of Mrs Nickleby's behaviour.)

Five years of Dickens's early life were spent at Chatham, between the ages of five and ten. These were happy years. Charles would go walking in the countryside with his father; one of their servants, Mary Weller, used to entertain him with

Left:
Elizabeth Dickens,
Charles's mother

Right:
Chatham, Kent in
the early
nineteenth century

Below:
Hungerford Stairs
on the River
Thames, with a
boot-blacking
factory shown on
the right

horrifying stories (Dickens later wrote about these in the piece 'Nurse's Stories', Chapter 15 in *The Uncommercial Traveller*); he went to school, learned to read, and then discovered a small collection of books in the attic of the house which he read repeatedly. One of his favourite books as a child was *The Arabian Nights*. He wrote about his childhood reading in Chapter 4 of *David Copperfield*.

(Years later, as a successful and established author, Dickens bought a house in the countryside near Chatham. It was a house that he and his father used to admire on their country walks together,

and his father had once told him that if he worked hard he might grow up to live in such a house.)

When the family left Chatham they moved to London, to a very modest house in Bayham Street, Camden Town. The family were in a lot of financial trouble. Charles was no longer sent to school, and soon started work in a warehouse, pasting labels onto pots of boot-polish. Shortly afterwards John Dickens was arrested for debt and the family had to go and live with him in the debtors' prison. Young Charles was found a room outside the prison where he lived, although he often visited his family. So, aged twelve, he found himself no longer in school, working in a very ordinary job and living virtually alone. He had had hopes of a bright future following a successful career at school, but these were all over, at least until his father somehow found the money to pay his debts which would enable the family to leave the prison and take up some more normal way of life.

Charles was a small, rather delicate looking boy and his workmates often bullied him and made fun of him. He was lonely and often hungry, and he had many worries. Although this situation only lasted a few weeks, it had a profound effect on Dickens. He wrote about his childhood experiences in the warehouse in Chapter 11 of *David Copperfield*.

The family lived in the Marshalsea Prison, which was unlike an ordinary prison. It was quite an easy-going place where debtors lived with their fami-

Left:
The Marshalsea
Prison, London

Below:
Wellington House
Academy, London

lies. But it operated an absurd system which made it all the more difficult for people to clear their debts, as they were unable to leave and find work until the debts had been paid! Dickens describes life in the Marshalsea in Chapters 6, 7, and 8 of *Little Dorrit*.

After a few weeks of imprisonment John Dickens inherited some money following his mother's death. This was enough to settle his debts and the family were free again. Charles was sent back to school, although he bitterly remembered that his mother would have preferred him to have stayed at work.

Charles spent the next three years at the Wellington House Academy in Camden Town, London. It was a school with a good reputation but Dickens claimed that he never learnt very much there, although he remembered a lot of caning going on. He wrote about a school similar to his own in Chapter 7 of *David Copperfield*.

At fifteen Charles left school and went to work in a solicitor's office. He found the work very dull, so, after teaching himself shorthand he found a more interesting job as a reporter in a law court. He soon earned a reputation as an accurate reporter and found another job reporting Parliamentary debates. He spent his leisure time going to the theatre as often as he could, and reading in the British

Museum Library. He nearly became an actor, but was ill on the day of his audition. Soon afterwards he started having some success with his journalism and so never tried again for the professional stage, although, as we shall see, he remained a keen amateur.

Dickens also spent the four years between the ages of seventeen and twenty-one hopelessly courting a pretty, lively girl called Maria Beadnell. They went through all the agonies of courtship – breaking up, reuniting, planning to marry, and so on – until she finally rejected him.

Maria Beadnell

Meanwhile, Dickens had met another girl, Catherine Hogarth, who was very unlike Maria. Catherine was a calm, loving, quiet sort of girl and many people have commented that Dickens became attached to her 'on the rebound'. They became engaged and, after the publication of *Sketches by Boz*, they were soon married.

Dickens the young journalist was more successful than Dickens the lover. He became a full-time political reporter for the *Morning Chronicle* in August 1834 and during that year and the next he started having short descriptive pieces published in a number of magazines and papers. He used the name 'Boz', which had been a pet-name of one of his brothers. Boz's pieces were noticed by the then-famous young author, William Harrison Ainsworth, who suggested to the unknown Dickens that he collect the pieces together and publish them in book form. Ainsworth also introduced Dickens to Macrone, a publisher, who brought out the book *Sketches by Boz* in February 1836.

Above:
Catherine Hogarth

Left:
Portrait of Dickens
as 'Boz'

Extracts from *Boz*

THE POOR CLERK

Dickens always wrote with great sympathy and understanding about ordinary people. This extract from his first book is a good example of his power of describing an ordinary person in an extraordinary way.

It is strange with how little notice, good, bad, or indifferent, a man may live and die in London. He awakens no sympathy in the breast of any single person; his existence is a matter of interest to no one save himself; he cannot be said to be forgotten when he dies, for no one remembered him when he was alive. There is a numerous class of people in this great metropolis who seem not to possess a single friend, and whom nobody appears to care for. Urged by imperative necessity in the first instance, they have resorted to London in search of employment, and the means of subsistence. . . . Old country friends have died or emigrated; former correspondents have become lost, like themselves, in the crowd and turmoil of some busy city: and they have gradually settled down into mere passive creatures of habit and endurance.

We were seated in the enclosure of St James's Park the other day, when our attention was attracted by a man whom we immediately put down in our own mind as one of this class. He was a tall, thin, pale person, in a black coat, scanty grey trousers, little pinched-up gaiters, and brown beaver gloves. He had an umbrella in his hand – not for use, for the day was fine – but, evidently, because he always carried one to the office in the morning. He walked up and down before the little patch of grass on which the chairs are placed for hire, not as if he were doing it for pleasure or recreation, but as if it were a matter of compulsion, just as he would walk to the office every morning from the back settlements of Islington. It was Monday; he had escaped for four-and-twenty hours from the thraldom of the desk; and was walking here for exercise and amusement – perhaps for the first time in his life. We were inclined to think he had never had a holiday before, and that he did not know what to do with himself. Children were playing on the grass; groups of people were loitering about, chatting and laughing; but the man walked steadily up and down, unheeding and unheeded, his spare pale face looking as if it were incapable of bearing the expression of curiosity or interest.

There was something in the man's manner and appearance which told us, we fancied, his whole life, or rather his whole day, for a man of this sort has no variety of days. We thought we almost saw the dingy little back office into which he walks every morning, hanging his hat on the same peg, and placing his legs beneath the same desk: first, taking off that black coat which lasts the year through, and putting on the one which did duty last year, and which he still keeps in his desk to save the other. There he sits till five o'clock, working on, all day, as regularly as the dial over the mantel-piece, whose loud ticking is as monotonous as his whole existence: only raising his head when some one enters the counting-house, or when, in the midst of some difficult calculation, he looks up to the ceiling as if there were inspiration in the dusty skylight with a green knot in the centre of every pane of glass. About five, or half-past, he slowly dismounts from his accustomed stool, and again changing his coat, proceeds to his usual dining-place, somewhere near Bucklersbury. The waiter recites the bill of fare in a rather confidential manner – for he is a regular customer – and after inquiring 'What's in the best cut?' and 'What was up last?' he orders a small plate of roast beef, with greens, and half-a-pint of porter. He has a small plate today, because greens are a penny more than potatoes, and he had 'two breads' yesterday, with the additional enormity of 'a cheese' the day before. This important point settled, he hangs up his hat – he took it off the moment he sat down – and bespeaks the paper after the next gentleman. If he can get it while he is at dinner, he eats with much greater zest; balancing it against the water-bottle, and eating a bit of beef, and reading a line or two, alternately. Exactly at five minutes before the hour is up, he produces a shilling, pays the reckoning, carefully deposits the change in his waistcoat-pocket (first deducting a penny for the waiter), and returns to the office, from which, if it is not foreign post night, he again sallies forth in about half an hour. He then walks home, at his usual pace, to his little back room at Islington, where he has his tea; perhaps solacing himself during the meal with the conversation of his landlady's little boy, whom he occasionally rewards with a penny, for solving problems in simple addition. Sometimes, there is a letter or two to take up to his

George Cruikshank

employer's, in Russell Square; and then, the wealthy man of business, hearing his voice, calls out from the dining-parlour, – 'Come in, Mr Smith': and Mr Smith, putting his hat at the feet of one of the hall chairs, walks timidly in, and being condescendingly desired to sit down, carefully tucks his legs under his chair, and sits at a considerable distance from the table while he drinks the glass of sherry which is poured out for him by the eldest boy, and after drinking which, he backs and slides out of the room, in a state of nervous agitation from which he does not perfectly recover, until he finds himself once more in the Islington Road. Poor, harmless creatures such men are; contented but not happy; broken-spirited and humbled, they may feel no pain, but they never know pleasure.

From *Sketches by Boz*, 'The Poor Clerk' from 'Thoughts about People'

WRITING

Dickens's technique here is to look closely at the person he is describing, comment on his or her appearance, and then imagine the life this person leads. (Note the details: he even imagines what vegetables the man eats!)
1 Try using the same technique to write your own 'sketch' of a stranger.
2 Describe the poor clerk's day off, or holiday, or evening out.

Another of the *Sketches* describes a street scene, in which two young girls, on their way from Bow Street Police Office to prison, attract the attention of a crowd who gather to watch them being loaded into the prisoners' van.

We were passing the corner of Bow Street, on our return from a lounging excursion the other afternoon, when a crowd, assembled round the door of the Police Office, attracted our attention. We turned up the street accordingly. There were thirty or forty people, standing on the pavement and half across the road; and a few stragglers were patiently stationed on the opposite side of the way – all evidently waiting in expectation of some arrival. We waited too, a few minutes, but nothing occurred: . . . a general exclamation from all the boys in the crowd of 'Here's the wan!' caused us to raise our heads, and look up the street.

The covered vehicle, in which prisoners are conveyed from the police offices to the different prisons was coming along at full speed . . .

The van drew up at the office-door, and the people thronged round the steps, just leaving a little alley for the prisoners to pass through . . . The driver, and another man who had been seated by his side in front of the vehicle, dismounted, and were admitted into the office. The office-door was closed after them, and the crowd were on the tiptoe of expectation.

After a few minutes' delay, the door again opened, and the two first prisoners appeared. They were a couple of girls, of whom the elder could not be more than sixteen, and the younger of whom had certainly not attained her fourteenth year. That they were sisters was evident from the resemblance which still subsisted between them, though two additional years of depravity had fixed their brand upon the elder girl's features, as legibly as if a red-hot iron had seared them. They were both gaudily dressed, the younger one especially; and, although there was a strong similarity between them in both respects, which was rendered the more obvious by their being handcuffed together, it is impossible to conceive a greater contrast than the demeanour of the two presented. The younger girl was weeping bitterly – not for display, or in the hope of producing effect, but for very shame; her face was buried in her handkerchief: and her whole manner was but too expressive of bitter and unavailing sorrow.

'How long are you for, Emily?' screamed a red-faced woman in the crowd. 'Six weeks and labour,' replied the elder girl with a flaunting laugh; 'and that's better than the stone jug anyhow; the mill's a deal better than the Sessions, and here's Bella-a-going too for the first time. Hold up your head, you chicken,' she continued, boisterously tearing the other girl's handkerchief away; 'Hold up your head, and show 'em your face. I an't jealous, but I'm blessed if I an't game!' – 'That's right, old gal,' exclaimed a man in a paper cap, who, in common with the greater part of the crowd, had been inexpressibly delighted with this little incident. – 'Right!' replied the girl; 'ah, to be sure; what's the odds, eh?' – 'Come! In with you,' interrupted the driver. 'Don't you be in a hurry, coachman,' replied the girl, 'and recollect I want to be set down in Cold Bath Fields – large house with a high garden-wall in front; you can't mistake it. Hallo! Bella, where are you going to – you'll pull my precious arm off!' This was addressed to the younger girl, who, in her anxiety to hide herself in the caravan, had ascended the steps first, and forgotten the strain upon the handcuff. 'Come down, and let's show you the way.' And after jerking the miserable girl down with a force which made her stagger on the pavement, she got into the vehicle, and was followed by her wretched companion.

These two girls had been thrown upon London streets, their vices and debauchery, by a sordid and rapacious mother. What the younger girl was then, the elder had been once; and what the elder then was, the younger must soon become. A melancholy prospect, but how surely to be realised; a tragic drama, but how often acted! Turn to the prisons and police offices of London – nay, look into the very streets themselves. These things pass before our eyes, day after day, and hour after hour – they have become such matters of course, that they are utterly disregarded. The progress of these girls in crime will be as rapid as the flight of a pestilence, resembling it too in its baneful influence and wide-spreading infection. Step by step, how many wretched females, within the sphere of every man's observation, have become involved in a career of vice, frightful to contemplate; hopeless at its commencement, loathsome and repulsive in its course; friendless, forlorn, and unpitied, at its miserable conclusion!

There were other prisoners – boys of ten, as hardened in vice as men of fifty – a houseless vagrant, going joyfully to prison as a place of food and shelter, handcuffed to a man whose prospects were ruined, character lost, and family rendered destitute, by his first offence. Our curiosity, however, was satisfied. The first group had left an impression on our mind we would gladly have avoided, and would willingly have effaced.

The crowd dispersed; the vehicle rolled away with its load of guilt and misfortune; and we saw no more of the Prisoners' Van.

From *Sketches by Boz*, 'The Prisoners' Van' from 'Characters', Ch. 12

FOR DISCUSSION

1 What differences does Dickens note between the characters of the two girls?
2 What explanation does he offer for their becoming criminals?
3 What does he mean by 'These things pass before our eyes, day after day, and hour after hour – they have become such matters of course, that they are utterly disregarded.'?
4 What reason might Dickens have had for writing this piece?
5 Write a conversation between the prisoners, once they are in the van.

Satire is when you mock something by exaggerating it, thereby making it look silly, and yet writing about it in a seemingly serious way. In the following extract Dickens satirises the early nineteenth-century passion for collecting information in statistical form.

THE MUDFOG ASSOCIATION

From 'Full Report of the First Meeting of the Mudfog Association for the Advancement of Everything'

'SECTION C. – STATISTICS.
HAY-LOFT, ORIGINAL PIG.

President – Mr Woodensconce. *Vice-Presidents* – Mr Ledbrain and Mr Timbered.

'MR SLUG stated to the section the result of some calculations he made with great difficulty and labour, regarding the state of infant education among the middle classes of London. He found that, within a circle of three miles from the Elephant and Castle, the following were the names and numbers of children's books principally in circulation:

Jack the Giant-killer	7,943
Ditto and Bean-stalk	8,621
Ditto and Eleven Brothers	2,845
Ditto and Jill	1,998
Total	21,407

'He found that the proportion of Robinson Crusoes to Philip Quarlls was as four and a half to one; and that the preponderance of Valentine and Orsons over Goody Two Shoeses was as three and an eighth of the former to half a one of the latter; a comparison of Seven Champions with Simple Simons gave the same result. The ignorance that prevailed was lamentable. One child, on being asked whether he would rather be Saint George of England or a respectable tallow-chandler, instantly replied, 'Taint George of Ingling'. Another, a little boy of eight years old, was found to be firmly impressed with a belief in the existence of dragons, and openly stated that it was his intention when he grew up, to rush forth sword in hand for the deliverance of captive princesses, and the promiscuous slaughter of giants. Not one child among the number interrogated had ever heard of Mungo Park*, – some inquiring whether he was at all connected with the black man that swept the crossing; and others whether he was in any way related to the Regent's Park. They had not the slightest conception of the commonest principles of mathematics, and considered Sinbad the Sailor the most enterprising voyager that the world had ever produced.

'A MEMBER strongly deprecating the use of all the other books mentioned, suggested that Jack and Jill might perhaps be exempted from the general censure, inasmuch as the hero and heroine, in the very outset of the tale, were depicted as going *up* a hill to fetch a pail of water, which was a laborious and useful occupation, –supposing the family linen was being washed, for instance.

'MR SLUG feared that the moral effect of this passage was more than counterbalanced by another in a subsequent part of the poem, in which very gross allusion was made to the mode in which the heroine was personally chastised by her mother

'"For laughing at Jack's disaster;"

besides, the whole work had this one great fault, *it was not true.*

'THE PRESIDENT complimented the honourable member on the excellent distinction he had drawn. Several other members, too, dwelt upon the immense and urgent necessity of storing the minds of children with nothing but facts and figures; which process the President very forcibly remarked, had made them (the section) the men they were.

*Mungo Park – a famous explorer.

FOR DISCUSSION

1 How can you tell that this is a satirical piece?
2 What point is Dickens making at the end about 'truth', 'facts' and 'figures'?

DRAMA SUGGESTION

Imagine a visit by members of the Mudfog Association to a school to collect some of this information. How would the teachers and pupils have responded?

Sketches by Boz was Dickens's big break; it put him firmly in the public eye and established him as a writer. The *Sketches* included a wide variety of pieces: detailed descriptions, social comment, reporting and satire. Dickens also included a number of comic stories, grouped together in the section 'Tales'. You might enjoy reading 'Sentiment', 'The Tuggses at Ramsgate' and 'The Bloomsbury Christening'.

'Boz' creates Pickwick

April 1836 was a special month for Dickens: he married Catherine, and also took on a challenging new literary task. Following the success of *Sketches by Boz* he was asked to write a series of comic stories based around a set of printed drawings on sporting subjects. These were to be published in monthly parts. The young author took control of the project and it became a runaway success. He was soon earning enough from his new publication to enable him to give up his job on the *Morning Chronicle* and to concentrate on writing fiction.

The new publication was called *The Pickwick Papers*. As it was published in monthly parts the author could tell from the sales figures which new developments were popular. When Dickens invented Sam Weller, the cheeky Cockney who becomes Mr Pickwick's man-servant, the sales figures soared. The reading public loved this new comic writer. (To some extent Dickens created his own readership through this technique of monthly publication: people who could not afford a large expensive book *could* afford a monthly part-issue. This meant that Dickens, throughout his career, had a very 'wide' readership in terms of social class.)

In the following extract from *The Pickwick Papers*, Mr Pickwick, Sam Weller and some of Mr Pickwick's friends – having been arrested on suspicion of duelling – are brought before Mr Jinks, the local magistrate.

Mr Pickwick and his freinds were conducted into the hall, whence, having been previously announced by Muzzle, and ordered in by Mr Nupkins, they were ushered into the worshipful presence of that public-spirited officer.

The scene was an impressive one, well calculated to strike terror to the hearts of culprits, and to impress them with an adequate idea of the stern majesty of the law. In front of a big book-case, in a big chair, behind a big table, and before a big volume, sat Mr Nupkins, looking a full size larger than any one of them, big as they were. The table was adorned with piles of papers: and above the further end of it, appeared the head and shoulders of Mr Jinks, who was busily engaged in looking as busy as possible. The party having all entered, Muzzle carefully closed the door, and placed himself behind his master's chair to await his orders. Mr Nupkins threw himself back, with thrilling solemnity, and scrutinised the faces of his unwilling visitors.

'Now, Grummer, who is that person?' said Mr Nupkins, pointing to Mr Pickwick, who, as the spokesman of his friends, stood hat in hand, bowing with the utmost politeness and respect.

'This here's Pickvick, your wash-up,' said Grummer.

'Come, none o' that 'ere, old Strike-a-light,' interposed Mr Weller, elbowing himself into the front rank. 'Beg your pardon, sir, but this here officer o' yourn in the gambooge tops, 'ull never earn a decent livin' as a master o' the ceremonies any vere. This here, sir,' continued Mr Weller, thrusting Grummer aside, and addressing the magistrate with pleasant familiarity, 'This here is S. Pickvick, Esquire; this here's Mr Tupman; that 'ere's Mr Snodgrass; and furder on, next him on the t'other side, Mr Winkle – all wery nice genl'm'n, sir, as you'll be wery happy to have the acquaintance on; so the sooner you commits these here officers o' yourn to the treadmill for a month or two, the sooner we shall begin to be on a pleasant understanding. Business first, pleasure arterwards, as King Richard the Third said wen he stabbed the t'other king in the Tower, afore he smothered the babbies.'

At the conclusion of this address, Mr Weller brushed his hat with his right elbow, and nodded benignly to Jinks, who had heard him throughout, with unspeakable awe.

'Who is this man, Grummer?' said the magistrate.

'Wery desp'rate ch'racter, your wash-up,' replied Grummer. 'He attempted to rescue the prisoners, and assaulted the officers; so we took him into custody, and brought him here.'

'You did quite right,' replied the magistrate. 'He is evidently a desperate ruffian.'

'He is my servant, sir,' said Mr Pickwick, angrily.

'Oh! he is your servant, is he?' said Mr Nupkins. 'A conspiracy to defeat the ends of justice, and murder its officers. Pickwick's servant. Put that down, Mr Jinks.'

Mr Jinks did so.

'What's your name, fellow?' thundered Mr Nupkins.

'Veller,' replied Sam.

'A very good name for the Newgate Calendar,' said Mr Nupkins.

This was a joke; so Jinks, Grummer, Dubbley, all the specials, and Muzzle, went into fits of laughter of five minutes' duration.

'Put down his name, Mr Jinks,' said the magistrate.

'Two L's, old feller,' said Sam.

Here an unfortunate special laughed again, whereupon the magistrate threatened to commit him, instantly. It is a dangerous thing to laugh at the wrong man, in these cases.

'Where do you live?' said the magistrate.

'Vare-ever I can,' replied Sam.

'Put down that, Mr Jinks,' said the magistrate, who was fast rising into a rage.

'Score it under,' said Sam.

'He is a vagabond, Mr Jinks,' said the magistrate. 'He is a vagabond on his own statement; is he not, Mr Jinks?'

'Certainly, sir.'

'Then I'll commit him. I'll commit him as such,' said Mr Nupkins.

'This is a wery impartial country for justice,' said Sam. 'There ain't a magistrate goin' as don't commit himself, twice as often as he commits other people.'

From *The Pickwick Papers*, Ch. 25, pp. 422–3

WRITING

Imagine the conversation between Mr Nupkins and a close friend on the evening following this trial. What do you think Mr Nupkins had to say about Sam? Write the conversation as a short play or as a dialogue. (This could be done with a partner and recorded.)

While Dickens was writing *The Pickwick Papers* he was appointed editor of a new magazine, *Bentley's Miscellany*. He not only edited it but started writing a new novel to be published in it: *Oliver Twist*. He also agreed with the publisher of *The Pickwick Papers* that he would start writing a new novel as soon as *Pickwick* was finished. He also wrote the occasional 'Sketch' for good measure. The young author's energetic output was interrupted briefly by a domestic tragedy. When he married Catherine her younger sister Mary had come and lived with the young couple. Dickens was very attached to his young sister-in-law and

Mary Hogarth

QUESTIONS

(for written answers and/or discussion)

1 Why does Dickens repeat the word 'big' in the second paragraph?

2 The phrases 'worshipful presence', 'stern majesty' and 'thrilling solemnity' all sound important and impressive. Is Dickens using them seriously or is he being ironic (mocking)?

3 Why does Sam Weller interrupt Grummer?

4 What is Mr Jinks's reaction to this interruption?

5 What does Grummer mean by 'your wash-up'? Why has Dickens written the phrase like this?

6 How would you describe Sam's attitude to the magistrate and the proceedings?

she lived with them for several months. Then, suddenly, she was taken ill and died in the course of two days. She died in Dickens's arms, and he was so grief-stricken that he could do no work. Both *Pickwick* and *Oliver Twist* – he was working on both at the time – missed their monthly instalments. Young Mary haunted Dickens's dreams for the rest of his life.

Three comic nasties

Dickens's great achievement was as a comic writer, although he wrote in many other veins as well – tragic, social, satirical, poetic. His books combine all these elements, but the comedy is what makes Dickens such an outstanding writer. Not all his comic characters were simply cheeky young men. Here are three comic 'nasties': Quilp, the dwarf bully from *The Old Curiosity Shop*; Mr Pecksniff from *Martin Chuzzlewit* and Uriah Heep from *David Copperfield*, two of Dickens's great hypocrites.

QUILP

Mr Quilp is a dwarf with a mischievous and powerful personality. Here we find him at breakfast. As usual he takes every opportunity of terrorising his wife and mother-in-law, Mrs Jiniwin.

'Mrs Quilp.'
'Yes, Quilp,' said the timid sufferer.
'Help your mother to get breakfast, Mrs Quilp. I am going to the wharf this morning – the earlier, the better, so be quick.'

Mrs Jiniwin made a faint demonstration of rebellion by sitting down in a chair near the door and folding her arms as if in resolute determination to do nothing. But a few whispered words from her daughter, and a kind inquiry from her son-in-law whether she felt faint, with a hint that there was abundance of cold water in the next apartment, routed these symptoms effectually, and she applied herself to the prescribed preparations with sullen diligence.

While they were in progress, Mr Quilp withdrew to the adjoining room and turning back his coat-collar, proceeded to smear his countenance with a damp towel of very unwholesome appearance, which made his complexion rather more cloudy than it was before.

But while he was thus engaged, his caution and inquisitiveness did not forsake him, for with a face as sharp and cunning as ever, he often stopped, even in this short process, and stood listening for any conversation in the next room, of which he might be the theme.

'Ah!' he said after a short effort of attention, 'it was not the towel over my ears, I thought it wasn't. I'm a little hunchy villain and a monster, am I, Mrs Jiniwin? Oh!'

The pleasure of this discovery called up the old doglike smile in full force. When he had quite done with it, he shook himself in a very doglike manner, and rejoined the ladies.

Mr Quilp now walked up to the front of a looking-glass, and was standing there putting on his neckerchief when Mrs Jiniwin, happening to be behind him, could not resist the inclination she felt to shake her fist at her tyrant son-in-law. It was the gesture of an instant, but as she did so and accompanied the action with a menacing look, she met his eye in the glass, catching her in the very act. The same glance at the mirror conveyed to her the reflection of a horribly grotesque and distorted face with the tongue lolling out; and the next instant the dwarf, turning about with a perfectly bland and placid look, inquired in a tone of great affection,

'How are you now, my dear old darling?'

Slight and ridiculous as the incident was, it made him appear such a little fiend, and withal such a keen and knowing one, that the old woman felt too much afraid of him to utter a single word, and suffered herself to be led with extraordinary politeness to the breakfast-table. Here he by no means diminished the impression he had just produced, for he ate hard eggs, shell and all, devoured gigantic prawns with the heads and tails on, chewed tobacco and water-cresses at the same time and with extraordinary greediness, drank boiling tea without winking, bit his fork and spoon till they bent again, and in short performed so many horrifying and uncommon acts that the women were nearly frightened out of their wits, and began to doubt if he were really a human creature. At last, having gone through these proceedings and many others which were equally a part of his system, Mr Quilp left them, reduced to a very obedient and humbled state, and betook himself to the riverside, where he took boat for the wharf on which he had bestowed his name.

From *The Old Curiosity Shop* Ch. 5, pp. 84–6

PECKSNIFF

Mr Pecksniff, a widower, is a religious phoney: he pretends to be charitable and pious but he is really

greedy, selfish and, as we shall see, rather lecher-
ous. Here he is making advances towards Mrs
Todgers, landlady of the boarding house where he
is staying with his two daughters.

'O h, Mrs Todgers!'
'My goodness!' exclaimed that lady.
'How low you are in your spirits, sir!'
'I am a man, my dear madam,' said Mr Pecksniff,
shedding tears, and speaking with an imperfect
articulation, 'but I am also a father. I am also a
widower. My feelings, Mrs Todgers, will not consent
to be entirely smothered, like the young children in
the Tower. They are grown up, and the more I press
the bolster on them, the more they look round the
corner of it.'

He suddenly became conscious of the bit of muffin,
and stared at it intently: shaking his head the while, in
a forlorn and imbecile manner, as if he regarded it as
his evil genius, and mildly reproached it.

'She was beautiful, Mrs Todgers,' he said, turning
his glazed eye again upon her, without the least
preliminary notice. 'She had a small property.'

'So I have heard,' cried Mrs Todgers with great
sympathy.

'Those are her daughters,' said Mr Pecksniff,
pointing out the young ladies, with increased emotion.

Mrs Todgers had no doubt of it.

'Mercy and Charity,' said Mr Pecksniff, 'Charity
and Mercy. Not unholy names, I hope?'

'Mr Pecksniff!' cried Mrs Todgers. 'What a ghastly
smile! Are you ill, sir?'

He pressed his hand upon her arm, and answered
in a solemn manner, and a faint voice, 'Chronic.'

'Cholic?' cried the frightened Mrs Todgers.

'Chron-ic,' he repeated with some difficulty.
'Chron-ic. A chronic disorder. I have been its victim
from childhood. It is carrying me to my grave.'

'Heaven forbid!' cried Mrs Todgers.

'Yes, it is,' said Mr Pecksniff, reckless with despair,
'I am rather glad of it, upon the whole. You are like
her, Mrs Todgers.'

'Don't squeeze me so tight, pray, Mr Pecksniff. If
any of the gentlemen should notice us.'

'For her sake,' said Mr Pecksniff. 'Permit me. In
honour of her memory. For the sake of a voice from
the tomb. You are *very* like her, Mrs Todgers! What a
world this is!'

'Ah! Indeed you may say that!' cried Mrs Todgers.

'I'm afraid it is a vain and thoughtless world,' said
Mr Pecksniff, overflowing with despondency. 'These
young people about us. Oh! what sense have they of
their responsibilities? None. Give me your other
hand, Mrs Todgers.'

That lady hesitated, and said 'she didn't like'.

'Has a voice from the grave no influence?' said Mr
Pecksniff, with dismal tenderness. 'This is irreligious!
My dear creature.'

'Hush!' urged Mrs Todgers. 'Really you mustn't.'

'It's not me,' said Mr Pecksniff. 'Don't suppose it's
me: it's the voice; its her voice.'

Mrs Pecksniff deceased, must have had an unusually thick and husky voice for a lady, and rather a stuttering voice, and to say the truth somewhat of a drunken voice, if it had ever borne much resemblance to that in which Mr Pecksniff spoke just then.

From *Martin Chuzzlewit*, Ch. 9, pp. 208–9

URIAH HEEP

Uriah Heep claims to be the most humble of men, but in fact he is a wicked, scheming, ambitious man who has realised that pretending to be humble is a good way to gain the approval of his superiors and so advance his career. He is a lawyer's clerk, and here we find him using his claims to humility to impress young David Copperfield, who has just joined the office.

'I suppose you are quite a great lawyer?' I said, after looking at him for some time.

'Me, Master Copperfield?' said Uriah. 'Oh, no! I'm a very umble person.'

It was no fancy of mine about his hands, I observed; for he frequently ground the palms against each other as if to squeeze them dry and warm, besides often wiping them, in a stealthy way, on his pocket-handkerchief.

'I am well aware that I am the umblest person going,' said Uriah Heep, modestly; 'let the other be where he may. My mother is likewise a very umble person. We live in a numble abode, Master Copperfield, but have much to be thankful for. My father's former calling was umble. He was a sexton.'

'What is he now?' I asked.

'He is a partaker of glory at present, Master Copperfield,' said Uriah Heep. 'But we have much to be thankful for. How much have I to be thankful for in living with Mr Wickfield!'

I asked Uriah if he had been with Mr Wickfield long?

'I have been with him, going on four year, Master Copperfield,' said Uriah; shutting up his book, after carefully marking the place where he had left off. 'Since a year after my father's death. How much have I to be thankful for, in that! How much have I to be thankful for, in Mr Wickfield's kind intention to give me my articles, which would otherwise not lay within the umble means of mother and self!'

'Then, when your articled time is over, you'll be a regular lawyer, I suppose?' said I.

'With the blessing of Providence, Master Copperfield,' returned Uriah.

'Perhaps you'll be a partner in Mr Wickfield's business, one of these days,' I said, to make myself

20. My father is a partaker of glory at present, Master Copperfield, but we have much to be thankful for.

Uriah Heep, taken from a series of late-Victorian cigarette cards, showing characters from Dickens's novels

agreeable; 'and it will be Wickfield and Heep, or Heep late Wickfield.'

'Oh no, Master Copperfield,' returned Uriah, shaking his head. 'I am much too umble for that!'

He certainly did look uncommonly like the carved face on the beam outside my window, as he sat, in his humility, eyeing me sideways, with his mouth widened, and the creases in his cheeks.

'Mr Wickfield is a most excellent man, Master Copperfield,' said Uriah. 'If you have known him long, you know it, I am sure, much better than I can inform you.'

I replied that I was certain he was; but that I had not known him long myself, though he was a friend of my aunt's.

'Oh, indeed, Master Copperfield,' said Uriah. 'Your aunt is a sweet lady, Master Copperfield!'

He had a way of writhing when he wanted to express enthusiasm, which was very ugly; and which diverted my attention from the compliment he had paid my relation, to the snaky twistings of his throat and body.

'A sweet lady, Master Copperfield!' said Uriah Heep. 'She has a great admiration for Miss Agnes, Master Copperfield, I believe?'

I said, 'Yes,' boldly; not that I knew anything about it, Heaven forgive me!

'I hope you have, too, Master Copperfield,' said Uriah. 'But I am sure you must have.'

'Everybody must have,' I returned.

'Oh, thank you, Master Copperfield,' said Uriah Heep, 'for that remark! It is so true! Umble as I am, I know it is so true! Oh, thank you, Master Copperfield!'

He writhed himself quite off his stool in the excitement of his feelings, and, being off, began to make arrangements for going home.

'Mother will be expecting me,' he said, referring to a pale, inexpressive-faced watch in his pocket, 'and getting uneasy; for though we are very umble, Master Copperfield, we are much attached to one another. If you would come and see us, any afternoon, and take a cup of tea at our lowly dwelling, mother would be as proud of your company as I should be.'

I said I should be glad to come.

'Thank you, Master Copperfield,' returned Uriah, putting his book away upon the shelf.

From *David Copperfield*, Ch. 16, pp. 291–2

ACTIVITIES

1 Illustrate one or more of these extracts.
2 Working in groups of two or three, prepare one of these extracts to be read aloud in a manner that brings out the humour and the characters involved. Tape your reading.
3 Write an extract yourself, using one of these comic nasties in a situation that brings out their full character.

Comic couples

Dickens also enjoyed writing humorously about love and lovers. Mr Pickwick, the bachelor hero of his first novel, gets into an awkward situation with Mrs Bardell, his widowed landlady, when he tries discussing his decision to employ a manservant. He has sent Mrs Bardell's son out with a message and then tries sharing his thoughts with her. Unfortunately, she misunderstands him.

It was evident that something of great importance was in contemplation, but what that something was, not even Mrs Bardell herself had been enabled to discover.

'Mrs Bardell,' said Mr Pickwick, at last, as that amiable female approached the termination of a prolonged dusting of the apartment—

'Sir,' said Mrs Bardell.

'Your little boy is a very long time gone.'

'Why it's a good long way to the Borough, sir,' remonstrated Mrs Bardell.

'Ah,' said Mr Pickwick, 'very true; so it is.'

Mr Pickwick relapsed into silence, and Mrs Bardell resumed her dusting.

'Mrs Bardell,' said Mr Pickwick, at the expiration of a few minutes.

'Sir,' said Mrs Bardell again.

'Do you think it a much greater expense to keep two people, than to keep one?'

'La, Mr Pickwick,' said Mrs Bardell, colouring up to the very border of her cap, as she fancied she observed a species of matrimonial twinkle in the eyes of her lodger; 'La, Mr Pickwick, what a question!'

'Well, but *do* you?' inquired Mr Pickwick.

'That depends—' said Mrs Bardell, approaching the duster very near to Mr Pickwick's elbow, which was planted on the table – 'that depends a good deal upon the person, you know, Mr Pickwick; and whether it's a saving and careful person, sir.'

'That's very true,' said Mr Pickwick, 'but the person I have in my eye (here he looked very hard at Mrs Bardell) I think possesses these qualities; and has, moreover, a considerable knowledge of the world, and a great deal of sharpness, Mrs Bardell; which may be of material use to me.'

'La, Mr Pickwick,' said Mrs Bardell; the crimson rising to her cap-border again.

'I do,' said Mr Pickwick, growing energetic, as was his wont in speaking of a subject which interested him, 'I do, indeed; and to tell you the truth, Mrs Bardell, I have made up my mind.'

'Dear me, sir,' exclaimed Mrs Bardell.

'You'll think it very strange now,' said the amiable Mr Pickwick, with a good-humoured glance at his companion, 'that I never consulted you about this matter, and never even mentioned it, till I sent your little boy out this morning – eh?'

Mrs Bardell could only reply by a look. She had long worshipped Mr Pickwick at a distance, but here she was, all at once, raised to a pinnacle to which her wildest and most extravagant hopes had never dared to aspire. Mr Pickwick was going to propose – a deliberate plan, too – sent her little boy to the Borough, to get him out of the way – how thoughtful – how considerate!

'Well,' said Mr Pickwick, 'what do you think?'

'Oh, Mr Pickwick,' said Mrs Bardell, trembling with agitation, 'you're very kind, sir.'

'It'll save you a good deal of trouble, won't it?' said Mr Pickwick.

'Oh, I never thought anything of the trouble, sir,' replied Mrs Bardell; 'and, of course, I should take more trouble to please you then, than ever; but it is so kind of you, Mr Pickwick, to have so much consideration for my loneliness.'

'Ah, to be sure,' said Mr Pickwick; 'I never thought of that. When I am in town, you'll always have somebody to sit with you. To be sure, so you will.'

'I'm sure I ought to be a very happy woman,' said Mrs Bardell.

'And your little boy—' said Mr Pickwick.

'Bless his heart!' interposed Mrs Bardell, with a maternal sob.

'He, too, will have a companion,' resumed Mr Pickwick, 'a lively one, who'll teach him, I'll be bound, more tricks in a week than he would ever learn in a year.' And Mr Pickwick smiled placidly.

'Oh you dear—' said Mrs Bardell.

Mr Pickwick started.

'Oh you kind, good, playful dear,' said Mrs Bardell; and without more ado, she rose from her chair, and flung her arms round Mr Pickwick's neck, with a cataract of tears and a chorus of sobs.

'Bless my soul,' cried the astonished Mr Pickwick;

– 'Mrs Bardell my good woman – dear me, what a situation – pray consider. – Mrs Bardell, don't – if anybody should come—'

'Oh, let them come,' exclaimed Mrs Bardell, frantically; 'I'll never leave you, – dear, kind, good, soul;' and, with these words, Mrs Bardell clung the tighter.

'Mercy upon me,' said Mr Pickwick, struggling violently, 'I hear somebody coming up the stairs. Don't, don't, there's a good creature, don't.' But entreaty and remonstrance were alike unavailing: for Mrs Bardell had fainted in Mr Pickwick's arms; and before he could gain time to deposit her on a chair, Master Bardell entered the room, ushering in Mr Tupman, Mr Winkle, and Mr Snodgrass.

From *The Pickwick Papers*, Ch. 12, pp. 230–32

FOR DISCUSSION

1 What does Mrs Bardell think Mr Pickwick is trying to discuss with her?

2 What does Mr Pickwick do or say to encourage Mrs Bardell's mistake?

3 What do you think Mr Pickwick tells his friends Tupman, Winkle and Snodgrass?

4 What do you think Mrs Bardell does when she wakes from her faint?

Mr Bumble, the pompous and scheming Parish Beadle in *Oliver Twist*, is not so confirmed a bachelor as Mr Pickwick. One cold winter's evening he calls in on Mrs Corney, the widowed Matron of the Workhouse, on an official errand. He is about to leave when Mrs Corney speaks up.

'Y ou'll have a very cold walk, Mr Bumble,' said the matron.

'It blows, ma'am,' replied Mr Bumble, turning up his coat-collar, 'enough to cut one's ears off.'

The matron looked, from the little kettle, to the beadle, who was moving towards the door; and as the beadle coughed, preparatory to bidding her good night, bashfully inquired whether – whether he wouldn't take a cup of tea?

Mr Bumble instantaneously turned back his collar again; laid his hat and stick upon a chair; and drew another chair up to the table. As he slowly seated himself, he looked at the lady. She fixed her eyes upon the little teapot. Mr Bumble coughed again, and slightly smiled.

Mrs Corney rose to get another cup and saucer from the closet. As she sat down, her eyes again encountered those of the gallant beadle; she coloured, and applied herself to the task of making his tea. Again Mr Bumble coughed, – louder this time than he had coughed yet.

'Sweet? Mr Bumble?' inquired the matron, taking up the sugar-basin.

'Very sweet, indeed, ma'am,' replied Mr Bumble. He fixed his eyes on Mrs Corney as he said this; and if ever a beadle looked tender, Mr Bumble was that beadle at that moment.

The tea was made, and handed in silence. Mr Bumble, having spread a handkerchief over his knees to prevent the crumbs from sullying the splendour of his shorts, began to eat and drink; varying these amusements, occasionally, by fetching a deep sigh; which, however, had no injurious effect upon his appetite, but, on the contrary, rather seemed to facilitate his operations in the tea and toast department.

'You have a cat, ma'am, I see,' said Mr Bumble, glancing at one who, in the centre of her family, was basking before the fire; 'and kittens, too, I declare!'

'I am so fond of them, Mr Bumble, you can't think,' replied the matron. 'They're *so* happy, *so* frolicsome, and *so* cheerful, that they are quite companions for me.'

'Very nice animals, ma'am,' replied Mr Bumble, approvingly; 'so very domestic.'

'Oh yes!' rejoined the matron with enthusiasm; 'so fond of their home too, that it's quite a pleasure, I'm sure.'

'Mrs Corney, ma'am,' said Mr Bumble, slowly, and marking the time with his teaspoon, 'I mean to say this, ma'am; that any cat, or kitten, that could live with you, ma'am, and *not* be fond of its home, must be a ass, ma'am.'

'Oh, Mr Bumble!' remonstrated Mrs Corney.

'It's of no use disguising facts, ma'am,' said Mr Bumble, slowly flourishing the teaspoon with a kind of amorous dignity which made him doubly impressive; 'I would drown it myself, with pleasure.'

'Then you're a cruel man,' said the matron vivaciously, as she held out her hand for the beadle's cup; 'and a very hard-hearted man besides.'

'Hard-hearted, ma'am?' said Mr Bumble. 'Hard?' Mr Bumble resigned his cup without another word; squeezed Mrs Corney's little finger as she took it; and inflicting two open-handed slaps upon his laced waistcoat, gave a mighty sigh, and hitched his chair a very little morsel farther from the fire.

It was a round table; and as Mrs Corney and Mr Bumble had been sitting opposite each other, with no space between them, and fronting the fire, it will be seen that Mr Bumble, in receding from the fire, and still keeping at the table, increased the distance between himself and Mrs Corney; which proceeding, some prudent readers will doubtless be disposed to admire, and to consider an act of great heroism on Mr Bumble's part: he being in some sort tempted by time, place, and opportunity, to give utterance to certain soft nothings, which however well they may become the lips of the light and thoughtless, do seem immeasurably beneath the dignity of judges of the land, members of parliament, ministers of state, lord mayors, and other great public functionaries, but more particularly beneath the stateliness and gravity of a beadle, who (as is well known) should be the sternest and most inflexible among them all.

Whatever were Mr Bumble's intentions, however (and no doubt they were of the best): it fortunately happened, as has been twice before remarked, that the table was a round one; consequently Mr Bumble, moving his chair by little and little, soon began to diminish the distance between himself and the matron; and, continuing to travel round the outer edge of the circle, brought his chair, in time, close to that in which the matron was seated. Indeed, the two chairs touched; and when they did so, Mr Bumble stopped.

Now, if the matron had moved her chair to the right, she would have been scorched by the fire; and if to the left, she must have fallen into Mr Bumble's arms; so (being a discreet matron, and no doubt

foreseeing these consequences at a glance) she remained where she was, and handed Mr Bumble another cup of tea.

'Hard-hearted, Mrs Corney?' said Mr Bumble, stirring his tea, and looking up into the matron's face; 'are *you* hard-hearted, Mrs Corney?'

'Dear me!' exclaimed the matron, 'what a very curious question from a single man. What can you want to know for, Mr Bumble?'

The beadle drank his tea to the last drop; finished a piece of toast; whisked the crumbs off his knees; wiped his lips; and deliberately kissed the matron.

'Mr Bumble!' cried the discreet lady in a whisper; for the fright was so great, that she had quite lost her voice, 'Mr Bumble, I shall scream!' Mr Bumble made no reply; but in a slow and dignified manner, put his arm round the matron's waist.

As the lady had stated her intention of screaming, of course she would have screamed at this additional boldness, but that the exertion was rendered unnecessary by a hasty knocking at the door: which was no sooner heard, than Mr Bumble darted, with much agility, to the wine bottles, and began dusting them with great violence: while the matron sharply demanded who was there. It is worthy of remark, as a curious physical instance of the efficacy of a sudden surprise in counteracting the effects of extreme fear, that her voice had quite recovered all its official asperity.

'If you please, mistress,' said a withered old female pauper, hideously ugly: putting her head in at the door, 'Old Sally is a-going fast.'

'Well, what's that to me?' angrily demanded the matron. 'I can't keep her alive, can I?'

'No, no, mistress,' replied the old woman, raising her hand, 'nobody can; she's far beyond the reach of help. I've seen a many people die; little babes and great strong men; and I know when death's a-coming,

well enough. But she's troubled in her mind: and when the fits are not on her – and that's not often, for she is dying very hard, – she says she has got something to tell, which you must hear. She'll never die till you come, mistress.'

At this intelligence, the worthy Mrs Corney muttered a variety of invectives against old women who couldn't even die without purposely annoying their betters; and, muffling herself in a thick shawl which she hastily caught up, briefly requested Mr Bumble to stay till she came back, lest anything particular should occur. Bidding the messenger walk fast, and not be all night hobbling up the stairs, she followed her from the room with a very ill grace, scolding all the way.

Mr Bumble's conduct on being left to himself, was rather inexplicable. He opened the closet, counted the teaspoons, weighed the sugar-tongs, closely inspected a silver milk-pot to ascertain that it was of the genuine metal, and, having satisfied his curiosity on these points, put on his cocked hat corner-wise, and danced with much gravity four distinct times round the table. Having gone through this very extraordinary performance, he took off the cocked hat again, and, spreading himself before the fire with his back towards it, seemed to be mentally engaged in taking an exact inventory of the furniture.

From *Oliver Twist*, Ch. 23, pp. 219–23

FOR DISCUSSION

1 Can you offer an explanation for Mr Bumble's 'rather inexplicable' behaviour when left alone?

2 What does Mr Bumble say to flatter Mrs Corney?

3 What do Mr Bumble and Mrs Corney have in common?

4 If this scene were acted out, which would be the funniest moments?

5 What do you think happened to these two lovebirds?

WRITING

Imagine Mr Bumble and Mrs Corney continue their courtship by post. Write a short series of love-letters between them. (As they are both Parish Officials, their letters may include some items of official business.)

In *Nicholas Nickleby* Dickens has some fun at the expense of the newly-wed Mr and Mrs Mantalini, a couple who run a fashionable dress-making establishment. Mrs Mantalini organizes the business while Mr Mantalini spends the money she makes on dressing up in flamboyant clothes. He talks and behaves in an equally showy manner. Ralph Nickleby, Nicholas and Kate's wicked uncle, has taken Kate to meet the Mantalinis, in order to help her find a job. Mr Mantalini is the first to meet them.

He was dressed in a gorgeous morning gown, with a waistcoat and Turkish trousers of the same pattern, a pink silk neckerchief, and bright green slippers, and had a very copious watch-chain wound round his body. Moreover, he had whiskers and a moustache, both dyed black and gracefully curled.

'Demmit, you don't mean to say you want me, do you, demmit?' said this gentleman, smiting Ralph on the shoulder.

'Not yet,' said Ralph, sarcastically.

'Ha! ha! demmit,' cried the gentleman; when wheeling round to laugh with greater elegance, he encountered Kate Nickleby, who was standing near.

'My niece,' said Ralph.

'I remember,' said the gentleman, striking his nose with the knuckle of his forefinger as a chastening for his forgetfulness. 'Demmit, I remember what you come for. Step this way, Nickleby; my dear, will you follow me? Ha! ha! They all follow me, Nickleby; always did, demmit, always.'

Giving loose to the playfulness of his imagination after this fashion, the gentleman led the way to a private sitting-room on the second floor scarcely less elegantly furnished than the apartment below, where the presence of a silver coffee-pot, an egg-shell, and sloppy china for one, seemed to show that he had just breakfasted.

'Sit down, my dear,' said the gentleman: first staring Miss Nickleby out of countenance, and then grinning in delight at the achievement.'This cursed high room takes one's breath away. These infernal sky parlours – I'm afraid I must move, Nickleby.'

'I would, by all means,' replied Ralph, looking bitterly round.

'What a demd rum fellow you are, Nickleby,' said the gentleman, 'the demdest, longest-headed, queerest-tempered old coiner of gold and silver ever was – demmit.'

Having complimented Ralph to this effect, the gentleman rang the bell, and stared at Miss Nickleby till it was answered, when he left off to bid the man desire his mistress to come directly; after which he began again, and left off no more till Madame Mantalini appeared.

The dress-maker was a buxom person, handsomely dressed and rather good-looking, but much older than the gentleman in the Turkish trousers, whom she had wedded some six months before. His name was originally Muntle; but it had been converted, by an easy transition, into Mantalini: the lady rightly considering that an English appellation would be of serious injury to the business. He had married on his whiskers, upon which property he had previously subsisted in a genteel manner for some years, and which he had recently improved after patient cultivation by the addition of a moustache, which promised to secure him an easy independence: his share in the labours of the business being at present confined to spending the money, and occasionally when that ran short, driving to Mr Ralph Nickleby to procure discount – at a percentage – for the customers' bills.

'My life,' said Mr Mantalini, 'what a demd devil of a time you have been!'

'I didn't even know Mr Nickleby was here, my love,' said Madame Mantalini.

'Then what a doubly demd infernal rascal that footman must be, my soul,' remonstrated Mr Mantalini.

'My dear,' said Madame, 'that is entirely your fault.'

'My fault, my heart's joy?'

'Certainly,' returned the lady; 'what can you expect, dearest, if you will not correct the man?'

'Correct the man, my soul's delight!'

'Yes; I am sure he wants speaking to, badly enough,' said Madame, pouting.

'Then do not vex itself,' said Mr Mantalini; 'he shall be horsewhipped till he cries out demnebly.' With this promise Mr Mantalini kissed Madame Mantalini, and after that performance Madame Mantalini pulled Mr Mantalini playfully by the ear, which done they descended to business.

'Now, ma'am,' said Ralph, who had looked on at all this, with such scorn as few men can express in looks, 'this is my niece.'

'Just so, Mr Nickleby,' replied Madame Mantalini, surveying Kate from head to foot and back again. 'Can you speak French, child?'

'Yes, ma'am,' replied Kate, not daring to look up; for she felt that the eyes of the odious man in the dressing-gown were directed towards her.

'Like a demd native?' asked the husband.

Miss Nickleby offered no reply to this inquiry, but turned her back upon the questioner, as if addressing herself to make answer to what his wife might demand.

'We keep twenty young women constantly employed in the establishment,' said Madame.

'Indeed, ma'am!' replied Kate, timidly.

'Yes; and some of 'em demd handsome, too,' said the master.

'Mantalini!' exclaimed his wife, in an awful voice.

'My senses' idol!' said Mantalini.

'Do you wish to break my heart?'

'Not for twenty thousand hemispheres populated with – with – with little ballet-dancers,' replied Mantalini in a poetical strain.

'Then you will, if you persevere in that mode of speaking,' said his wife. 'What can Mr Nickleby think when he hears you?'

From *Nicholas Nickleby*, Ch. 10, pp. 189–91

FOR DISCUSSION

1 What is the source of tension between Mr and Mrs Mantalini?
2 What pretence are they trying to keep up in public?

DRAMA SUGGESTIONS

1 Continue the argument between Mr and Mrs Mantalini. Try to use similarly artificial compliments and far-fetched pet-names.
2 Much of the comedy in these extracts lies in the way the characters talk to each other. In groups of three – narrator and the comic couple – prepare one of these extracts for reading aloud in a manner that brings the comedy alive.

2

Charles Dickens and his times

The New Poor Law

Before 1834 very poor people could be helped in two different ways:

1 *Indoor relief* – The old, sick, mad, crippled and orphaned were fed and housed in their local **workhouse**.
2 *Outdoor relief* – unemployed or underpaid workers and the temporarily sick were given money for food and rent by local officials.

In 1834 the Government approved the New Poor Law, which meant that Outdoor Relief was *not* given to 'able-bodied paupers' – those we would now call the unemployed. Under this law they only received Indoor Relief in their local workhouse.

To discourage people from settling for the workhouse rather than taking a job, the standard of living in the workhouse (food, heating, clothing, bedding and so on) was *below* that of the lowest paid worker. The Government intended that this would keep those who *could* work *out* of the workhouse and would reduce the cost of running it. Families who entered the workhouse were split up, so married couples lived apart, and children were separated from their parents.

This system was very unpopular with the poor, who felt that the workhouse was, in effect, a place where they were punished for being poor. However, the ratepayers liked the new system, as it kept down their taxes, and employers found that workers would accept very low wages rather than go into the workhouse.

Dickens opens his second novel, *Oliver Twist* (written 1837–8), in a workhouse. Young Oliver returns there from the 'baby farm', where he has spent his first nine years, on the same day that local officials decide to change from the old system to the new one. As a result, Dickens can make some remarks of his own about the effects of the New Poor Law.

Poor Oliver! He little thought, as he lay sleeping in a happy unconsciousness of all around him, that the board had that very day arrived at a decision which would exercise the most material influence over all his future fortunes. But they had. And this was it:

The members of this board were very sage, deep, philosophical men, and when they came to turn their attention to the workhouse, they found out at once, what ordinary folks would never have discovered – the poor people liked it! It was a regular place of public entertainment for the poorer classes; a tavern where there was nothing to pay; a public breakfast, dinner, tea and supper all the year round; a brick and mortar elysium [heaven], where it was all play and no work. 'Oho!' said the board, looking very knowing; 'we are the fellows to set this to rights; we'll stop it all, in no time.' So, they established the rule, that all poor people should have the alternative (for they could compel nobody, not they), of being starved by a gradual process in the house, or by a quick one out of it. With this view, they contracted with the water-works to lay on an unlimited supply of water; and with a corn-factor to supply periodically small quantities of oatmeal; and issued three meals of thin gruel a day, with an onion twice a week, and half a roll on Sundays. They made a great many other wise and humane regulations having reference to the ladies, which it is not necessary to repeat; kindly undertook to divorce poor married people, in consequence of the great expense of a suit in Doctors' Commons [the court that dealt, very expensively, with divorces]; and, instead of compelling a man to support his family, as they had theretofore done, took his family away from him, and made him a bachelor! There is no saying how many applicants for relief, under these last two heads, might have started up in all classes of society, if it had not been coupled with the workhouse; but the board were long-headed men, and had provided for this difficulty. The relief was inseparable from the workhouse and the gruel; and that frightened people.

For the first six months after Oliver Twist was removed, the system was in full operation. It was rather expensive at first, in consequence of the increase in the undertaker's bill, and the necessity of taking in the clothes of all the paupers, which fluttered loosely on their wasted, shrunken forms, after a week or two's gruel. But the number of workhouse inmates got thin as well as the paupers; and the board were in ecstasies.

From *Oliver Twist*, Ch. 2, pp. 54–5

Vagrants in the casual ward of a workhouse in the mid-nineteenth century (from a sketch)

FOR DISCUSSION

1 What criticisms is Dickens making here of the New Poor Law?
2 In what tone does he make these criticisms? – is he angry? amused? outraged? sarcastic?

ACTIVITIES

1 Read on:
   Chapters 2 and 3 about Oliver's life at the hands of the local officials.
2 Find out about:
   (a) *Poverty then*: The New Poor Law; Edwin Chadwick, chief administrator of the Poor Law; Pauper apprentices.
   (b) *Poverty now*: Unemployment benefit and Social Security – why two systems? How are orphans and widows cared for in our society? What does the term 'poverty line' mean? Is it still a crime to be poor? What attitudes can one find in the media towards the unemployed and to families living on social security? Who is to blame for unemployment?

   Information sources:
   Child Poverty Action Group, 1 Macklin Street, London WC2 (01-242-9149)
   NSPCC, 67 Saffron Hill, London, EC1 (01-242-1626)

The Yorkshire schools

In *Nicholas Nickleby*, the novel published immediately after *Oliver Twist*, Dickens turns his critical eye on the Yorkshire Schools. Two or three days' journey by stage-coach from London, these notorious boarding schools were to be found in the northern part of Yorkshire. Many people knew they were a racket, and were run purely to make profits for their owners. Illegitimate, deformed or retarded children were often sent there as a cheap means of keeping them hidden to avoid embarrassment to their parents. Other parents with not much money were sometimes deceived by advertisements for these schools, and thought that they were a genuine way of buying a good education at a bargain price.

The schools advertised in newspapers, and often included the phrase 'No Vacations' to show parents who wished to be rid of unwanted children that they provided this special service. The children were housed and fed as cheaply as possible. They were taught very little, and many became ill – some became blind or even died from neglect.

Nicholas Nickleby, hero of the novel, is forced by his wicked Uncle Ralph to teach at Dotheboys Hall, run by Mr Squeers and his wife. After a long and uncomfortable journey north, and a bad night's sleep, Nicholas enters the schoolroom on his first morning.

He could not but observe how silent and sad the boys all seemed to be. There was none of the noise and clamour of a school-room, none of its boisterous play or hearty mirth. The children sat crouching and shivering together, and seemed to lack the spirit to move about. The only pupil who evinced the slightest tendency towards locomotion or playfulness was Master Squeers, and as his chief amusement was to tread upon the other boys'

toes in his new boots, his flow of spirits was rather disagreeable than otherwise.

After some half-hour's delay, Mr Squeers reappeared, and the boys took their places and their books, of which latter commodity the average might be about one to eight learners. A few minutes having elapsed, during which Mr Squeers looked very profound, as if he had a perfect apprehension of what was inside all the books, and could say every word of their contents by heart if he only chose to take the trouble, that gentleman called up the first class.

Obedient to his summons there ranged themselves in front of the schoolmaster's desk, half a dozen scarecrows, out at knees and elbows, one of whom placed a torn and filthy book beneath his learned eye.

'This is the first class in English spelling and philosophy, Nickleby,' said Squeers, beckoning Nicholas to stand behind him. 'We'll get up a Latin one, and hand that over to you. Now, then, where's the first boy?'

'Please, sir, he's cleaning the back parlour window,' said the temporary head of the philosophical class.

'So he is, to be sure,' rejoined Squeers. 'We go upon the practical mode of teaching, Nickleby; the regular education system. C-l-e-a-n, clean, verb active, to make bright, to scour. W-i-n, win, d-e-r, der, winder, a casement. When the boy knows this out of the book, he goes and does it. It's just the same principle as the use of the globes. Where's the second boy?'

'Please, sir, he's weeding the garden,' replied a small voice.

'To be sure,' said Squeers, by no means disconcerted. 'So he is. B-o-t, bot, t-i-n, tin, bottin, n-e-y, ney, bottinney, noun substantive, a knowledge of plants. When he has learned that bottinney means a knowledge of plants, he goes and knows 'em. That's our system, Nickleby: what do you think of it?'

'It's a very useful one, at any rate,' answered Nicholas significantly.

'I believe you,' rejoined Squeers, not remarking the emphasis of his usher. 'Third boy, what's a horse?'

'A beast, sir,' replied the boy.

'So it is,' said Squeers. 'Ain't it, Nickleby?'

'I believe there is no doubt of that, sir,' answered Nicholas.

'Of course there isn't,' said Squeers. 'A horse is a quadruped, and quadruped's Latin for beast, as everybody that's gone through the grammar knows, or else where's the use of having grammars at all?'

'Where, indeed!' said Nicholas abstractedly.

'As you're perfect in that,' resumed Squeers, turning to the boy, 'go and look after *my* horse, and rub him down well, or I'll rub you down. The rest of the class go and draw water up, till somebody tells you to leave off, for it's washing day tomorrow, and they want the coppers filled.'

So saying, he dismissed the first class to their experiments in practical philosophy, and eyed Nicholas with a look half cunning and half doubtful, as if he were not altogether certain what he might think of him by this time.

'That's the way we do it, Nickleby,' he said, after a pause.

Nicholas shrugged his shoulders in a manner that was scarcely perceptible, and said he saw it was.

'And a very good way it is, too,' said Squeers. 'Now, just take them fourteen little boys and hear them some reading, because, you know, you must begin to be useful. Idling about here won't do.'

Mr Squeers said this, as if it had suddenly occurred to him, either that he must not say too much to his assistant, or that his assistant did not say enough to him in praise of the establishment. The children were arranged in a semicircle round the new master, and he was soon listening to their dull, drawling, hesitating recital of those stories of engrossing interest which are to be found in the more antiquated spelling books.

In this exciting occupation the morning lagged heavily on.

From *Nicholas Nickleby*, Ch. 8, pp. 154–6

FOR DISCUSSION

1 How does Dickens get across to us that Squeers is a fraud?
2 What does Nicholas mean, when he says of Squeers's system, 'It's a very useful one, at any rate'?
3 What attitudes do people have today towards handicapped children? Do we still want them 'out of sight, out of mind'?

WRITING

1 Imagine you are a pupil at Dotheboys Hall. Your parents have sent you there thinking it is a good school. You decide that the best way of getting help is to smuggle a letter to them. Write the letter describing your life at the school.
2 Devise a short play about the arrival of a new boy. Your play should include an interview with Mr Squeers.

FURTHER READING

Chapters 7, 8, 9, 13, for more about Nicholas and Mr Squeers.

The growth of factories and towns

England started to become an industrialised country in the second half of the eighteenth century. By the time Dickens started writing, London, the West Midlands and the North of England were already industrial areas.

COTTAGE INDUSTRY

At first, most industries were organised on a small scale. Individual workers and their families would operate small machines, often in their own homes. The work was often done to add to the money the family earned as farm workers. Industry and the population were scattered over wide areas. Much machinery was *water-powered*, and had to be sited on fast-flowing rivers and streams. The early cotton-mills were frequently built in the heart of the countryside. This stage of development is often described as 'cottage industry'.

THE GROWTH OF FACTORIES

The development of *steam-powered* machinery meant that industry came to rely on larger, more efficient and more expensive machinery. It did not need swift rivers, and could be housed in factories built where there were roads or canals available to distribute the goods produced. It made better sense to build a factory in a town rather than in a remote corner of the countryside.

It soon became obvious that it was cheaper to produce goods in one large factory than in a number of scattered workshops. As such factories were more efficient and could produce more goods per worker than individual workshops, the price of factory-produced goods came down, so cottage-industry workers had to lower their rates

A needle-mill in
Worcestershire,
mid-nineteenth
century

of pay in order to compete. This soon proved a losing battle, and cottage workers began to give up trying to earn money at home. Large numbers left their homes to find work in the factories of the nearby towns.

This process is clearly seen in the following details of the weaving industry:

Year	Home weavers	Factory weavers	Total production (in million lbs)
1830	230,000	50,000	150
1845	60,000	150,000	300
1860	10,000	200,000	650
1880	(none)	250,000	1,000

(*Source*: R J Cruikshank, *Charles Dickens and Early Victorian England*, (London 1949), chart 13.)

THE GROWTH OF TOWNS

Small towns grew very rapidly with this concentration of industry and workers, and the growth was often unplanned. There were hardly any proper drains or adequate supplies of water to the houses, which were built as quickly and cheaply as possible for the incoming workers. Local government, where it existed, was often unable to cope with the sudden growth of the towns, and many of them did not have a Member of Parliament. Some were not even recognised as towns, and so no one accepted responsibility for things like street cleaning, policing, or providing and maintaining basic services such as roads.

In *The Old Curiosity Shop*, written 1840–41, Dickens describes a journey through a landscape between two neighbouring industrial towns.

On every side, as far as the eye could see into the heavy distance, tall chimneys, crowding on each other, and presenting that endless repetition of the same dull, ugly form, which is the horror of oppressive dreams, poured out their plague of smoke, obscured the light, and made foul the melancholy air. On mounds of ashes by the wayside, sheltered only by a few rough boards, or rotten penthouse roofs, strange engines spun and writhed like tortured creatures; clanking their iron chains, shrieking in their rapid whirl from time to time as though in torment unendurable, and making the ground tremble with their agonies. Dismantled houses here and there appeared, tottering to the earth, propped up by fragments of others that had fallen down, unroofed, windowless, blackened, desolate, but yet inhabited. Men, women, children, wan in their looks and ragged in attire, tended the engines, fed their tributary fires, begged upon the road, or scowled half-naked from the doorless houses. Then came more of the wrathful monsters, whose like they almost seemed to be in their wildness and their untamed air, screeching and turning round and round again; and still, before, behind, and to the right and left, was the same interminable perspective of brick towers, never ceasing in their black vomit, blasting all things living or inanimate, shutting out the face of day, and closing in on all these horrors with a dense dark cloud.

From *The Old Curiosity Shop*, Ch. 45, pp. 423–4

Dickens never specifies what these 'engines' are producing, but we have little difficulty understanding his feelings about the area.

Riot

The growing population in these unplanned, badly administered towns created enormous problems. Apart from bad housing and frequent bouts of infectious disease, there were also periods of unemployment which often forced people into the workhouse. The poor did not have the vote, and so there was little chance of their complaints being directly represented by a Member of Parliament.

During Dickens's lifetime a number of serious riots occurred in London and other cities. In the late 1830s the **Chartist** movement found a huge following among the urban workers, and there were many large demonstrations in support of the People's Charter. (Most of them were peaceful demonstrations despite their size.)

The movement started in 1835, when the General Working-Men's Association of London drew up a six-point charter for the reform of Parliament. The Charter demanded:

1 universal sufferage (votes for all men over 21);
2 annual parliaments;
3 payment of MPs – so that poor men could become MPs;
4 voting by secret ballot – to prevent intimidation by landlords and employers;
5 equal electoral districts – so that all areas had their fair share of MPs;
6 abolition of the need for candidates to own £300 worth of land – so that ordinary people could stand for election.

The agitation in favour of the Charter reached its peaks in 1839 and 1842. The campaign was linked with others against the New Poor Law and in favour of the Ten Hours Bill – a proposal to limit factory working hours (men, women and children frequently worked twelve, fourteen or even sixteen hours a day). Working people had many grievances, and their demonstrations were often multipurpose events. In Manchester in 1842, for example, there was a general strike for higher wages *and* for the Charter.

Strikes and demonstrations were always threatening and sometimes violent – a few degenerated into riots. These were put down with great violence by troops. In 1839 in Newport, South Wales, troops killed fourteen and wounded fifty Chartist demonstrators.

Dickens, although firmly on the side of the poor against the New Poor Law, was like many fellow writers very much against mass demonstrations and violent action. In his novel *Barnaby Rudge* (written 1841) he describes a mob's progress through London. Although he is writing about a particular set of riots from sixty years before (the Gordon Riots), he was clearly writing for his own time as well.

One other circumstance is worthy of remark; and that is, that from the moment of their first outbreak at Westminster, every symptom of order or preconcerted arrangement among them vanished. When they divided into parties and ran to different quarters of the town, it was on the spontaneous suggestion of the moment. Each party swelled as it went along, like rivers as they roll towards the sea; new leaders sprang up as they were wanted, disappeared when the necessity was over, and reappeared at the next crisis. Each tumult took shape and form from the circumstances of the moment; sober workmen, going home from their day's labour, were seen to cast down their baskets of tools and become rioters in an instant; mere boys on errands did the like. In a word, a moral plague ran through the city. The noise, and hurry, and excitement, had for hundreds and hundreds an attraction they had no firmness to resist. The contagion spread like a dread fever: an infectious madness, as yet not near its height, seized on new victims every hour, and society began to tremble at their ravings.

From *Barnaby Rudge*, Ch. 53, pp. 483–4

Indeed, the sense of having gone too far to be forgiven, held the timid together no less than the bold. Many who would readily have pointed out the foremost rioters and given evidence against them, felt that escape by that means was hopeless, when their every act had been observed by scores of people who had taken no part in the disturbances; who had suffered in their persons, peace, or property, by the outrages of the mob; who would be most willing witnesses; and whom the government would, no doubt, prefer to any King's evidence that might be offered. Many of this class had deserted their usual occupations on the Saturday morning; some had been seen by their employers active in the tumult; others knew they must be suspected, and that they would be discharged if they returned; others had been desperate from the beginning, and comforted themselves with the homely proverb, that, being hanged at all, they might as well be hanged for a sheep as a lamb. They all hoped and believed, in a greater or less degree, that the government they seemed to have paralysed, would, in its terror, come to terms with them in the end, and suffer them to make their own conditions. The least sanguine among them reasoned with himself that, at the worst, they were too many to be all punished, and that he had as good a chance of escape as any other man. The great mass never reasoned or thought at all, but were stimulated by their own headlong passions, by poverty, by ignorance, by the love of mischief, and the hope of plunder.

WRITING

1 What, according to this passage, stimulated the mass of rioters?
2 What other reasons are given for the mob sticking together?
3 'Each party swelled as it went along, like rivers as they roll towards the sea.' What ideas or pictures does this sentence create in your mind?
4 Comment on the meaning of 'a moral plague ran through the city'. How is this idea developed in the final two sentences of the extract?

FOR DISCUSSION

1 What evidence is there in this passage of Dickens's opposition to the mob?
2 What do you think Dickens's attitude would have been to modern demonstrations and marches?
3 What are your feelings about crowds? Have you ever been caught up in one? Was it frightening or exciting? Where did it happen? (Pop concert, football match, political demonstration, picket?)

Dickens wrote about riots again in his later novel, *A Tale of Two Cities*. As in *Barnaby Rudge*, the riots are set in the past, during the French Revolution of 1789. Here Dickens re-creates the moment when the mob storms the Bastille, the old fortress prison in Paris.

'Come, then!' cried Defarge, in a resounding voice. 'Patriots and friends, we are ready! The Bastille!'

With a roar that sounded as if all the breath in France had been shaped into the detested word, the living sea rose, wave on wave, depth on depth, and overflowed the city to that point. Alarm-bells ringing, drums beating, the sea raging and thundering on its new beach, the attack begun.

Deep ditches, double drawbridge, massive stone walls, eight great towers, cannon, muskets, fire and smoke. Through the fire and through the smoke – in the fire and in the smoke, for the sea cast him up against a cannon, and on the instant he became a cannonier – Defarge of the wine-shop worked like a manful soldier, Two fierce hours.

Deep ditch, single drawbridge, massive stone walls, eight great towers, cannon, muskets, fire and smoke. One drawbridge down! 'Work, comrades all, work! Work, Jacques One, Jacques Two, Jacques One Thousand, Jacques Two Thousand, Jacques Five-and-Twenty Thousand; in the name of all the Angels or the Devils – which you prefer – work!' Thus Defarge of the wine-shop, still at his gun, which had long grown hot.

'To me, women!' cried madame his wife. 'What! We can kill as well as the men when the place is taken!' And to her, with a shrill thirsty cry, trooping women variously armed, but all armed alike in hunger and revenge.

Cannon, muskets, fire and smoke; but, still the deep ditch, the single drawbridge, the massive stone walls, and the eight great towers. Slight displacements of the raging sea, made by the falling wounded. Flashing weapons, blazing torches, smoking waggon-loads of wet straw, hard work at neighbouring barricades in all directions, shrieks, volleys, execrations, bravery without stint, boom, smash and rattle, and the furious sounding of the living sea; but, still the deep ditch, and the single drawbridge, and the massive stone walls, and the eight great towers, and still Defarge of the wine-shop at his gun, grown doubly hot by the service of Four fierce hours.

A white flag from within the fortress, and a parley – this dimly perceptible through the raging storm, nothing audible in it – suddenly the sea rose immeasurably wider and higher, and swept Defarge of the wine-shop over the lowered drawbridge, past the massive stone outer walls, in among the eight great towers surrendered!

So resistless was the force of the ocean bearing him on, that even to draw his breath or turn his head was as impracticable as if he had been struggling in the surf at the South Sea, until he was landed in the outer court-yard of the Bastille. There, against an angle of a wall, he made a struggle to look about him. Jacques Three was nearly at his side; Madame Defarge, still heading some of her women, was visible in the inner distance, and her knife was in her hand. Everywhere was tumult, exultation, deafening and maniacal bewilderment, astounding noise, yet furious dumb-show.

'The Prisoners!'
'The Records!'
'The secret cells!'
'The instruments of torture!'
'The Prisoners!'

Of all these cries, and ten thousand incoherencies, 'The Prisoners!' was the cry most taken up by the sea that rushed in, as if there were an eternity of people, as well as of time and space. When the foremost billows rolled past, bearing the prison officers with them, and threatening them all with instant death if any secret nook remained undisclosed, Defarge laid his strong hand on the breast of one of these men – a man with a grey head, who had a lighted torch in his hand – separated him from the rest, and got him between himself and the wall.

'Show me the North Tower!' said Defarge. 'Quick!'

From *A Tale of Two Cities*, Ch. 21, pp. 245–6

FOR DISCUSSION OR WRITING

1 What techniques does Dickens use in this extract to convey the speed and movement of the crowd?
2 A **metaphor** is where one thing is described in terms of another. In this scene one particular metaphor is used many times.
  (a) What is the metaphor used in this passage?
  (b) What ideas does the metaphor suggest?
  (c) What is the effect of repeating it several times?

Campaigning and demonstrating continued to break out over various issues during Dickens's lifetime. Twenty-five years after *Barnaby Rudge* the cartoon shown below appeared in *Punch*, following a demonstration in London's Hyde Park by workers campaigning to get the vote.

RUFFIANLY POLICEMAN
ABOUT TO PERPETRATE A BRUTAL AND DASTARDLY ASSAULT ON THE PEOPLE.

FOR DISCUSSION

1 What point is the caption making?
2 What does the drawing itself suggest about the artist's attitude to the crowd of demonstrators?

Railway mania

Railway building started in the late 1820s, and by 1842 there were 2000 miles of track. Over the next eight years *three times* that amount of track was built. The financial investment peaked during the months of 'railway mania' in 1847. Suddenly everyone wanted to invest in this new system of transport.

Dickens was writing *Dombey and Son* (1846–8) during the time of railway mania, and in the novel he writes about the arrival of the railways. In Chapter 15, Walter, a young man, searches for a family who had lived in Staggs's Gardens, in London's Camden Town. However . . .

There was no such place as Staggs's Gardens. It had vanished from the earth. Where the old rotten summer-houses once had stood, palaces now reared their heads, and granite columns of gigantic girth opened a vista to the railway world beyond. The miserable waste ground, where the refuse-matter had been heaped of yore, was swallowed up and gone; and in its frowsy stead were tiers of warehouses, crammed with rich goods and costly merchandise. The old by-streets now swarmed with passengers and vehicles of every kind: the new streets that had stopped disheartened in the mud and waggon-ruts, formed towns within themselves, originating wholesome comforts and conveniences belonging to themselves, and never tried nor thought of until they sprung into existence. Bridges that had led to nothing, led to villas, gardens, churches, healthy public walks. The carcasses of houses, and beginnings of new thoroughfares, had started off upon the line at steam's own speed, and shot away into the country in a monster train.

. . . There were railway patterns in its drapers' shops, and railway journals in the windows of its newsmen. There were railway hotels, office-houses, lodging-houses, boarding-houses; railway plans, maps, views, wrappers, bottles, sandwich-boxes, and time-tables; railway hackney-coach and cab-stands; railway omnibuses, railway streets and buildings, railway hangers-on and parasites, and flatterers out of all calculation. There was even railway time observed in clocks, as if the sun itself had given in. Among the vanquished was the master chimney-sweeper, whilom incredulous at Staggs's Gardens, who now lived in a stuccoed house three stories high, and gave himself out, with golden flourishes upon a varnished board, as contractor for the cleansing of railway chimneys by machinery.

To and from the heart of this great change, all day and night, throbbing currents rushed and returned incessantly like its life's blood. Crowds of people and mountains of goods, departing and arriving scores upon scores of times in every four-and-twenty hours, produced a fermentation in the place that was always in action. The very houses seemed disposed to pack up and take trips. Wonderful Members of Parliament, who, little more than twenty years before, had made themselves merry with the wild railroad theories of engineers, and given them the liveliest rubs in cross-examination, went down into the north with their watches in their hands, and sent on messages before by the electric telegraph, to say that they were coming. Night and day the conquering engines rumbled at

their distant work, or, advancing smoothly to their journey's end, and gliding like tame dragons into the allotted corners grooved out to the inch for their reception, stood bubbling and trembling there, making the walls quake, as if they were dilating with the secret knowledge of great powers yet unsuspected in them, and strong purposes not yet achieved.

From *Dombey and Son*, Ch. 15, pp. 289–90

FOR DISCUSSION

1 What evidence is there in this passage of Dickens's enthusiasm and support for the railways?
2 What 'improvements' has this particular railway brought to this particular area?

WRITING

The modern equivalent of this disruption is the effect of motorway building, or a large flyover or underpass. Imagine you have returned to an area you once knew well to find it changed in such a way. Write a paragraph describing your feelings about what you see.

Building the retaining wall at Camden Town, London for the London & Birmingham Railway, 1838, a water-colour by C. Bourne

COKETOWN

The effect of the railways on an already industrialised country was to speed up the rate at which the economy developed. It suddenly became possible to distribute huge amounts of goods quickly, cheaply and reliably. This in turn meant that it made even better business sense to build factories that produced huge amounts of goods *in one place*, which were then distributed by rail to the different parts of the country. These processes are called *mass production* and *mass distribution.*

As the railways spread they carried with them cheap, mass-produced goods, which undercut the prices charged by local craftsmen who had traditionally produced goods for sale in their own shops. Local hat-makers, saddle-makers and eventually shoemakers and tailors all found themselves struggling to survive the competition of goods produced in far-away factories. Many went out of business, or became shop-keepers, selling factory-produced goods.

Thus the railways speeded up the change from cottage industry and craft industry to factory production. As the railways spread, so more and more factories were built and the amount of goods produced increased enormously.

One effect of the economy developing in this way was the emergence of single-industry towns. Although London and the Midlands had many different industries, other parts of the country developed into areas dominated by one or two major industries. Lancashire became the home of the cotton-spinning and weaving industries, and the West Riding of Yorkshire became the centre of the wool trade. The vast quantities of goods produced were transported not only to all corners of Britain but all over the world.

Dickens describes one such town in his book *Hard Times* (1854), where he invented Coketown. He based his invention on Preston in particular and on Lancashire towns in general. He had visited the cotton area because there had been a great deal of industrial strife, and he came away with a clear picture of the towns, their people and their values.

C oketown . . . was a triumph of fact. . . . It was a town of red brick, or of brick that would have been red if the smoke and ashes had allowed it; but, as matters stood it was a town of unnatural red and black like the painted face of a savage. It was a town of machinery and tall chimneys, out of which interminable serpents of smoke trailed themselves for ever and ever, and never got uncoiled. It had a black canal in it, and a river that ran purple with ill-smelling dye, and vast piles of building full of windows where there was a rattling and a trembling all day long, and where the piston of the steam-engine worked monotonously up and down, like the head of an elephant in a state of melancholy madness. It contained several large streets all very like one another, and many small streets still more like one another, inhabited by people equally like one another, who all went in and out at the same hours, with the same sound upon the same pavements, to do the same work, and to whom every day was the same as yesterday and tomorrow, and every year the counterpart of the last and the next.

These attributes of Coketown were in the main inseparable from the work by which it was sustained; against them were to be set off, comforts of life which found their way all over the world, and elegancies of life which made, we will not ask how much of the fine lady, who could scarcely bear to hear the place mentioned. The rest of its features were voluntary, and they were these.

You saw nothing in Coketown but what was severely workful. If the members of a religious persuasion built a chapel there – as the members of eighteen religious persuasions had done – they made it a pious warehouse of red brick, with sometimes (but this only in highly ornamented examples) a bell in a bird-cage on the top of it. The solitary exception was the New Church; a stuccoed edifice with a square steeple over the door, terminating in four short pinnacles like florid wooden legs. All the public inscriptions in the town were painted alike, in severe characters of black and white. The jail might have been the infirmary, the infirmary might have been the jail, the town-hall might have been either, or both, or anything else, for anything that appeared to the contrary in the graces of their construction. Fact, fact, fact, everywhere in the material aspect of the town; fact, fact, fact, everywhere in the immaterial. The M'Choakumchild school was all fact, and the school of design was all fact, and the relations between master and man were all fact, and everything was fact between the lying-in hospital and the cemetery, and what you couldn't state in figures, or show to be purchaseable in the cheapest market and saleable in the dearest, was not, and never should be, world without end, Amen.

From *Hard Times*, Book the First, Ch. 5, pp. 65–6

FOR DISCUSSION

1 What do you learn from this passage about the way of life in Coketown?
2 How does Dickens tell us that Coketown is an internationally important manufacturing town?
3 What do you think Dickens means by 'severely workful'?
4 What do you think Dickens is getting at with his phrase 'Fact, fact, fact . . .'?

FURTHER READING

You can find out more about 'Fact' and the M'Choakumchild school in Chapters 1 and 2 of *Hard Times*.

Dickens's criticisms of Coketown were wide-ranging. He thought that the way of life for the factory workers, the quality of the education offered in the schools, the grim architecture and the harsh relationships between employer and worker all had the effect of crushing the human imagination and freedom of spirit.

Look carefully at the picture below:

1 Do you think the painter feels the same way as Dickens about life in a factory town?
2 How is the picture similar to Dickens's description?
3 How does it differ from Dickens's description?

Clearly both painter and writer were responding to the same challenge: that of describing a new way of life and a new type of town.

'Dinner hour,
Wigan', a painting
by Eyre Crowe

Amusements

Dickens was firmly convinced of the value of public amusements. This idea became stronger and more important to him as he grew older. In his early novels he writes with a lot of affection about poor people's outings to circuses, waxworks and cheap theatres. In *The Old Curiosity Shop* Nell, the young heroine, meets Mrs Jarley, the owner of a travelling waxworks exhibition, who employs Nell to help run the show. They set up the wax models and Mrs Jarley then sets about teaching Nell the stories that she will have to recite to the public about each of the figures.

'That,' said Mrs Jarley in her exhibition tone, as Nell touched a figure at the beginning of the platform, 'is an unfortunate Maid of Honour in the Time of Queen Elizabeth, who died from pricking her finger in consequence of working upon a Sunday. Observe the blood which is trickling from her finger; also the gold-eyed needle of the period, with which she is at work.'

All this Nell repeated twice or thrice, pointing to the finger and the needle at the right times, and then passed on to the next.

'That, ladies and gentlemen,' said Mrs Jarley, 'is Jasper Packlemerton of atrocious memory, who courted and married fourteen wives, and destroyed them all by tickling the soles of their feet when they was sleeping in the concsiousness of innocence and virtue. On being brought to the scaffold and asked if he was sorry for what he had done, he replied yes, he was sorry for having let 'em off so easy, and hoped all Christian husbands would pardon him the offence. Let this be a warning to all young ladies to be particular in the character of the gentlemen of their choice. Observe that his finger is curled as if in the act of tickling, and that his face is represented with a wink, as he appeared when committing his barbarous murders.'

When Nell knew all about Mr Packlemerton, and could say it without faltering, Mrs Jarley passed on to the fat man, the tall man, and then to the thin man, the short man, the old lady who died of dancing at a hundred and thirty-two, the wild boy of the woods, the woman who poisoned fourteen families with pickled walnuts, and other historical characters and interesting but misguided individuals. And so well did Nell profit by her instructions, and so apt was she to remember them, that by the time they had been shut up together for a couple of hours, she was in full possession of the history of the whole establishment, and perfectly competent to the enlightenment of visitors.

From *The Old Curiosity Shop*, Ch. 26, pp. 283–5

FOR DISCUSSION

1 Why do the stories have to be recited to the public, rather than written on labels as at a modern waxworks?
2 What is particularly effective about Mrs Jarley's style of storytelling?
3 How would you describe Dickens's attitude to the waxworks?
4 Waxworks are still very popular. Enormous numbers of people still visit such famous waxworks as Madame Tussaud's or the London Dungeon. What is their appeal?

<table>
</table>

WRITING

Write a publicity leaflet for Mrs Jarley's waxworks. Include some of the details given in the extract, and try to write in a suitably crowd-pulling style.

The *rightness* of people's desire for entertainment became a political issue in the 1850s when there was strong opposition from religious pressure groups to such innocent pleasures as the Sunday-opening of the National Gallery and the British Museum in London. Sunday was, of course, the only day of the week that working people had to enjoy themselves. In 1852, the company that ran the Crystal Palace (an industrial exhibition opened in London in 1851) wanted to open its doors on Sundays, but the Government was persuaded by religious leaders not to allow it.

In 1855 a Bill was introduced into Parliament to stop *all* trading on Sundays and, during June and July, there were three huge demonstrations in London's Hyde Park against the Bill. Working people were furious: it was as if the Government were actively seeking to spoil their one day of leisure.

In *Little Dorrit*, which Dickens started in 1855, there is a moment when he makes clear where he stands on the issue of what is right and proper for a Sunday.

It was a Sunday evening in London, gloomy, close and stale. Maddening church bells of all degrees of dissonance, sharp and flat, cracked and clear, fast and slow, made the brick and mortar echoes hideous. Melancholy streets in a penitential garb of soot, steeped the souls of the people who were condemned to look at them out of windows, in dire despondency. In every thoroughfare, up almost every alley, and down almost every turning, some doleful bell was throbbing, jerking, tolling, as if the Plague were in the city and the dead-carts were going round. Everything was bolted and barred that could by possibility furnish relief to an overworked people. No pictures, no unfamiliar animals, no rare plants or flowers, no natural or artificial wonders of the ancient world – all *taboo* with that enlightened strictness, that the ugly South sea gods in the British Museum might have supposed themselves at home again. Nothing to see but streets, streets, streets. Nothing to breathe but streets, streets, streets. Nothing to change the brooding mind, or raise it up. Nothing for the spent toiler to do, but to compare the monotony of his seventh day with the monotony of his six days, think what a weary life he led, and make the best of it – or the worst, according to the probabilities.

From *Little Dorrit*, Ch. 3, pp. 67–8

As Mr Sleary, the lisping circus master in *Hard Times* said to the disapproving gentleman:

'Don't be croth with uth poor vagabondth. People mutht be amuthed. They can't be alwayth a learning, nor yet they can't be alwayth a working, they an't made for it. You *muth* have uth, Thquire. Do the withe thing and the kind thing too, and make the betht of uth; not the wurtht! . . .'

From *Hard Times*, Book 3, Ch. 8, p. 308

FOR DISCUSSION

The British Sunday – is it still a dull and depressing day? Could it be improved? What have you noticed about Sundays in other countries?

FIND OUT ABOUT

1 The Lord's Day Observance movement.
2 Popular amusements in the mid-nineteenth century.

Dickens's times were, as we have seen, harsh, exciting and rapidly changing. During his lifetime the cities expanded, the factory system flourished, the railways boomed, the new-style workhouse was established, and while many old cruelties were swept away many new ones appeared.

FURTHER READING

1 *Bleak House*, Chapter 1, on the old court of Chancery.
2 *Little Dorrit*, Chapter 10, for a view of the Civil Service.
3 *Our Mutual Friend*, Chapter 2, for Dickens's view of snobs.

3

An introduction to 'Great Expectations'

In this chapter we will take a close look at a particular novel. The whole story will not be given away, as I hope you will become sufficiently interested to go away and read the whole thing for yourself. *Great Expectations* was Dickens's second-to-last novel. The story is told from the point of view of Pip, an orphan, raised by his sister and her husband Joe, a blacksmith. Pip and his sister and brother-in-law live out on the Kent marshes, near where Dickens lived as a boy. The novel focuses closely on Pip himself, his childhood and adolescence, and on the influence upon him of the powerful characters he meets as he grows up.

The book starts when Pip is a child. He opens the novel by explaining how he formed an impression of his parents by studying their graves.

As I never saw my father or my mother, and never saw any likeness of either of them (for their days were long before the days of photographs), my first fancies regarding what they were like, were unreasonably derived from their tombstones. The shape of the letters on my father's, gave me an odd idea that he was a square, stout, dark man, with curly black hair. From the character and turn of the inscription, '*Also Georgiana Wife of the Above,*' I drew a childish conclusion that my mother was freckled and sickly. To five little stone lozenges, each about a foot and a half long, which were arranged in a neat row beside their grave, and were sacred to the memory of five little brothers of mine – who gave up trying to get a living exceedingly early in that universal struggle – I am indebted for a belief I religiously entertained that they had all been born on their backs with their hands in their trousers-pockets, and had never taken them out in this state of existence.

From Chapter 1, p. 35

---

1 What shape would the letters on the tombstone have been (line 6)?
2 What might have suggested to Pip that his mother was 'freckled and sickly' (lines 11–12)?
3 Why might Pip have formed such an impression about his little brothers (lines 18–21)?
4 What is Dickens exploring in this extract about our childhood imagination? Can you recall any similar memories from when you were a young child?

While Pip is in the graveyard, one winter afternoon, he is suddenly and terrifyingly surprised.

'Hold your noise!' cried a terrible voice, as a man started up from among the graves at the side of the church porch. 'Keep still, you little devil, or I'll cut your throat!'

A fearful man, all in coarse grey, with a great iron on his leg. A man with no hat, and with broken shoes, and with an old rag tied round his head. A man who had been soaked in water, and smothered in mud, and lamed by stones, and cut by flints, and stung by nettles, and torn by briars; who limped and shivered, and glared and growled; and whose teeth chattered in his head as he seized me by the chin.

From Chapter 1, p. 36

---

1 What does Pip immediately notice about the man?
2 What do you notice about these two sentences:

   'A fearful man, all in coarse grey, with a great iron on his leg.'
   'A man with no hat, and with broken shoes, and with an old rag tied round his head.'

Why do you think Dickens uses this style? What does it convey about Pip's feelings?

The man is desperate for food and, on learning that Pip's brother-in-law is a blacksmith, demands that Pip brings him a metal file as well as food, so that he can remove his leg-iron.

'You bring me, tomorrow morning early, that file and them wittles. You bring the lot to me, at that old Battery over yonder. You do it, and you never dare to say a word or dare to make a sign concerning your having seen such a person as me, or any person sumever, and you shall be let to live. You fail, or you go from my words in any partickler, no matter how small it is, and your heart and liver shall be tore out, roasted and ate. Now, I ain't alone, as you may think I am. There's a young man hid with me, in comparison with which young man I am a Angel. That young man hears the words I speak. That young man has a secret way pecooliar to himself, of getting at a boy, and at his heart, and at his liver. It is in wain for a boy to attempt to hide himself from that young man. A boy may lock his door, may be warm in bed, may tuck himself up, may draw the clothes over his head, may think himself comfortable and safe, but that young man will softly creep and creep his way to him and tear him open. I am keeping that young man from harming of you at the present moment, with great difficulty. I find it wery hard to hold that young man off of your inside. Now, what do you say?'

I said that I would get him the file, and I would get him what broken bits of food I could, and I would come to him at the Battery, early in the morning.

'Say, Lord strike you dead if you don't!' said the man.

I said so and he took me down.

'Now,' he pursued, 'you remember what you've undertook, and you remember that young man, and you get home!'

'Goo-good night, sir,' I faltered.

'Much of that!' said he, glancing about him over the cold wet flat. 'I wish I was a frog. Or a eel!'

At the same time, he hugged his shuddering body in both his arms – clasping himself, as if to hold himself together – and limped towards the low church wall. As I saw him go, picking his way among the nettles, and among the brambles that bound the green mounds, he looked in my young eyes as if he were eluding the hands of the dead people, stretching up cautiously out of their graves, to get a twist upon his ankle and pull him in.

From Chapter 1, pp. 37–38

The convict threatens Pip. (From the 1947 film *Great Expectations*)

1 What is so frightening about the man's threat (lines 17–22)?
2 Why might the man say 'I wish I was a frog. Or a eel!' (lines 38–39)?
3 Why might the man's movements seem to Pip 'as if he were eluding the hands of the dead people' (lines 46–47)?
4 While the man is obviously trying to frighten Pip, is Dickens trying to frighten his readers?

The next morning Pip brings the food as promised, which the man eats ravenously.

Pitying his desolation, and watching him as he settled down upon the pie, I made bold to say, 'I am glad you enjoy it.'
'Did you speak?'
'I said, I was glad you enjoyed it.' 5
'Thankee, my boy. I do.'
I had often watched a large dog of ours eating his food; and I now noticed a decided similarity between the dog's way of eating, and the man's. The man took strong sharp sudden bites, just like 10 the dog. He swallowed, or rather snapped up, every mouthful, too soon and too fast; and he looked sideways here and there while he ate, as if he thought there was danger in every direction of somebody's coming to take the pie away. He was 15 altogether too unsettled in his mind over it, to appreciate it comfortably, I thought, or to have anybody to dine with him, without making a chop with his jaws at the visitor. In all of which particulars he was very like the dog. 20

From Chapter 3, pp. 50–51

1 Why does Pip think the man eats like a dog?
2 How can you tell that Dickens is describing a child's thoughts?

PIP AND THE CONVICT
The man Pip encounters in the graveyard turns out to be an escaped convict. This encounter proves very important to them both. We have a lot in the above passages about Pip's impressions of the convict. What impressions do you think the convict has of Pip? How would he feel towards Pip at this point? What sort of memories would he have of Pip in the future?

Another strand to Pip's tale is the story of Estella and Miss Havisham. Pip meets them when Miss Havisham arranges through his uncle, Mr Pumblechook, for Pip to come and visit her. She lives in a large house and is known to be eccentric, although very few people have actually seen her in recent years. Pumblechook is keen to oblige this wealthy local eccentric and so goes along with her request to send a child to visit her.

Pip is met at the gate of the house by a girl, Estella, who shows him in.

'But don't loiter, boy.'
Though she called me 'boy' so often, and with a carelessness that was far from complimentary, she was of about my own age. She seemed much older than I, of course, 5 being a girl, and beautiful and self-possessed; and she was as scornful of me as if she had been one-and-twenty, and a queen.
We went into the house by a side door – the great front entrance had two chains across it 10 outside – and the first thing I noticed was, that the passages were all dark, and that she had left a candle burning there. She took it up, and we went through more passages and up a staircase, and still it was all dark, and only the candle lighted us. 15
At last we came to the door of a room, and she said, 'Go in.'
I answered, more in shyness than politeness, 'After you, miss.'
To this, she returned: 'Don't be ridiculous, 20 boy; I am not going in.' And scornfully walked away, and – what was worse – took the candle with her.
This was very uncomfortable, and I was half afraid. However, the only thing to be done being 25 to knock at the door, I knocked, and was told from within to enter. I entered, therefore, and found myself in a pretty large room, well lighted with wax candles. No glimpse of daylight was to be seen in it. It was a dressing-room, as I supposed 30 from the furniture, though much of it was of forms and uses then quite unknown to me. But prominent in it was a draped table with a gilded looking-glass, and that I made out at first sight to be a fine lady's dressing-table. 35
Whether I should have made out this object so soon, if there had been no fine lady sitting at it, I cannot say. In an arm-chair, with an elbow resting on the table and her head leaning on that hand, sat the strangest lady I have ever seen, or shall 40 ever see.

She was dressed in rich materials – satins, and lace, and silks – all of white. Her shoes were white. And she had a long white veil dependent from her hair, and she had bridal flowers in her hair, but her hair was white. Some bright jewels sparkled on her neck and on her hands, and some other jewels lay sparkling on the table. Dresses, less splendid than the dress she wore, and half-packed trunks, were scattered about. She had not quite finished dressing, for she had but one shoe on – the other was on the table near her hand – her veil was but half arranged, her watch and chain were not put on, and some lace for her bosom lay with those trinkets, and with her handkerchief, and gloves, and some flowers, and a Prayer-book, all confusedly heaped about the looking-glass.

It was not in the first few moments that I saw all these things, though I saw more of them in the first moments than might be supposed. But, I saw that everything within my view which ought to be white, had been white long ago, and had lost its lustre, and was faded and yellow. I saw that the bride within the bridal dress had withered like the dress, and like the flowers, and had no brightness left but the brightness of her sunken eyes. I saw that the dress had been put upon the rounded figure of a young woman, and that the figure upon which it now hung loose, had shrunk to skin and bone. Once I had been taken to see some ghastly waxwork at the Fair, representing I know not what impossible personage lying in state. Once, I had been taken to one of our old marsh churches to see a skeleton in the ashes of a rich dress, that had been dug out of a vault under the church pavement. Now, waxwork and skeleton seemed to have dark eyes that moved and looked at me. I should have cried out, if I could.

'Who is it?' said the lady at the table.

'Pip, ma'am.'

'Pip?'

'Mr Pumblechook's boy, ma'am. Come – to play.'

'Come nearer; let me look at you. Come close.'

It was when I stood before her, avoiding her eyes, that I took note of the surrounding objects in detail, and saw that her watch had stopped at twenty minutes to nine, and that a clock in the room had stopped at twenty minutes to nine.

'Look at me,' said Miss Havisham. 'You are not afraid of a woman who has never seen the sun since you were born?'

I regret to state that I was not afraid of telling the enormous lie comprehended in the answer 'No.'

'Do you know what I touch here?' she said, laying her hands, one upon the other, on her left side.

'Yes, ma'am.' (It made me think of the young man.)

'What do I touch?'

'Your heart.'

'Broken!'

She uttered the word with an eager look, and with strong emphasis, and with a weird smile that had a kind of boast in it. Afterwards, she kept her hands there for a little while, and slowly took them away as if they were heavy.

'I am tired,' said Miss Havisham. 'I want diversion, and I have done with men and women. Play.'

I think it will be conceded by my most disputatious reader, that she could hardly have directed an unfortunate boy to do anything in the wide world more difficult to be done under the circumstances.

'I sometimes have sick fancies,' she went on, 'and I have a sick fancy that I want to see some play. There, there!' with an impatient movement of the fingers of her right hand; 'play, play, play!'

For a moment, with the fear of my sister's working me before my eyes, I had a desperate idea of starting round the room in the assumed character of Mr Pumblechook's chaise-cart. But, I felt myself so unequal to the performance that I gave it up, and stood looking at Miss Havisham in what I suppose she took for a dogged manner, inasmuch as she said, when we had taken a good look at each other:

'Are you sullen and obstinate?'

'No, ma'am, I am very sorry for you, and very sorry I can't play just now. If you complain of me I shall get into trouble with my sister, so I would do it if I could; but it's so new here, and so strange, and so fine – and melancholy —' I stopped, fearing I might say too much, or had already said it, and we took another look at each other.

Before she spoke again, she turned her eyes from me, and looked at the dress she wore, and at the dressing-table, and finally at herself in the looking-glass.

'So new to him,' she muttered, 'so old to me; so strange to him, so familiar to me; so melancholy to both of us! Call Estella.'

As she was still looking at the reflection of herself, I thought she was still talking to herself, and kept quiet.

'Call Estella,' she repeated, flashing a look at me. 'You can do that. Call Estella. At the door.'

To stand in the dark in a mysterious passage of

an unknown house, bawling Estella to a scornful young lady neither visible nor responsive, and feeling it a dreadful liberty so to roar out her name, was almost as bad as playing to order. But, 155 she answered at last, and her light came along the dark passage like a star.

Miss Havisham beckoned her to come close, and took up a jewel from the table, and tried its effect upon her fair young bosom and against her 160 pretty brown hair. 'Your own, one day, my dear, and you will use it well. Let me see you play cards with this boy.'

'With this boy! Why, he is a common labouring-boy!' 165

I thought I overheard Miss Havisham answer – only it seemed so unlikely – 'Well? You can break his heart.'

'What do you play, boy?' asked Estella of myself, with the greatest disdain. 170

'Nothing but beggar my neighbour, Miss.'

'Beggar him,' said Miss Havisham to Estella. So we sat down to cards.

It was then I began to understand that everything in the room had stopped, like the watch and 175 the clock, a long time ago. I noticed that Miss Havisham put down the jewel exactly on the spot from which she had taken it up. As Estella dealt the cards, I glanced at the dressing-table, and saw that the shoe upon it, once white, now yellow, had 180 never been worn. I glanced down at the foot from which the shoe was absent, and saw that the silk stocking on it, once white, now yellow, had been trodden ragged. Without this arrest of everything, this standing still of all the pale decayed objects, 185 not even the withered bridal dress on the collapsed form could have looked so like grave-clothes, or the long veil so like a shroud.

So she sat, corpse-like, as we played at cards; the frillings and trimmings on her bridal dress, 190 looking like earthy paper. I knew nothing then of the discoveries that are occasionally made of bodies buried in ancient times, which fall to powder in the moment of being distinctly seen; but I have often thought since, that she must have 195 looked as if the admission of the natural light of the day would have struck her to dust.

'He calls the knaves, Jacks, this boy!' said Estella with disdain, before our first game was out. 'And what coarse hands he has! And what 200 thick boots!'

I had never thought of being ashamed of my hands before; but I began to consider them a very indifferent pair. Her contempt for me was so strong, that it became infectious, and I caught it. 205

She won the game, and I dealt. I misdealt, as was only natural, when I knew she was lying in wait for me to do wrong; and she denounced me for a stupid, clumsy labouring-boy.

'You say nothing of her,' remarked Miss 210 Havisham to me, as she looked on. 'She says many hard things of you, yet you say nothing of her. What do you think of her?'

'I don't like to say,' I stammered.

'Tell me in my ear,' said Miss Havisham, 215

Pip tells Miss Havisham what he thinks of Estella. (From the 1947 film *Great Expectations*)

48

bending down.

'I think she is very proud,' I replied, in a whisper.

'Anything else?'

'I think she is very pretty.'   220

'Anything else?'

'I think she is very insulting.' (She was looking at me then with a look of supreme aversion.)

'Anything else?'

'I think I should like to go home.'   225

'And never see her again, though she is so pretty?'

'I am not sure that I shouldn't like to see her again, but I should like to go home now.'

'You shall go soon,' said Miss Havisham aloud.   230
'Play the game out.'

Saving for the one weird smile at first, I should have felt almost sure that Miss Havisham's face could not smile. It had dropped into a watchful and brooding expression – most likely when all   235
the things about her had become transfixed – and it looked as if nothing could ever lift it up again. Her chest had dropped, so that she stooped; and her voice had dropped, so that she spoke low, and with a dead lull upon her; altogether, she had the   240
appearance of having dropped, body and soul, within and without, under the weight of a crushing blow.

I played the game to an end with Estella, and she beggared me. She threw the cards down on   245
the table when she had won them all, as if she despised them for having been won of me.

From Chapter 8, pp. 86–91

---

1 Why does Miss Havisham remind Pip of both a waxwork and a skeleton (lines 77–78)?

2 Why should it be so difficult for Pip to 'play' (line 112)?

3 What does Pip's comparison between Miss Havisham and ancient bodies suggest to you (lines 191–197)?

4 Why does Estella comment on Pip's language, hands and boots (lines 198–201)?

5 What does Pip mean by 'Her contempt for me was so strong, that it became infectious, and I caught it' (lines 204–205)?

6 What effect does Dickens achieve by having Pip repeat 'I think . . .' at the beginning of each answer (lines 217–225)?

7 Why do you think Miss Havisham may have taken to living in this way?

8 Do you think Pip's meeting with Estella might have a lasting effect on him?

When Pip returns home from Miss Havisham's he is questioned by his sister and Pumblechook about his visit.

'Now, boy! What was she a doing of, when you went in today?' asked Mr Pumblechook.

'She was sitting,' I answered, 'in a back velvet coach.'   5

Mr Pumblechook and Mrs Joe stared at one another – as they well might – and both repeated, 'In a black velvet coach?'

'Yes,' said I. 'And Miss Estella – that's her niece, I think – handed her in cake and wine at the   10
coach-window, on a gold plate. And we all had cake and wine on gold plates. And I got up behind the coach to eat mine, because she told me to.'

'Was anybody else there?' asked Mr Pumblechook.   15

'Four dogs,' said I.

'Large or small?'

'Immense,' said I. 'And they fought for veal-cutlets out of a silver basket.'

Mr Pumblechook and Mrs Joe stared at one   20
another again, in utter amazement. I was perfectly frantic – a reckless witness under the torture – and would have told them anything.

'Where *was* this coach, in the name of gracious?' asked my sister.   25

'In Miss Havisham's room.' They stared again. 'But there weren't any horses to it.' I added this saving clause, in the moment of rejecting four richly caparisoned coursers, which I had had wild thoughts of harnessing.   30

'Can this be possible, uncle?' asked Mrs Joe. 'What can the boy mean?'

'I'll tell you, Mum,' said Mr Pumblechook. 'My opinion is, it's a sedan-chair. She's flighty, you know – very flighty – quite flighty enough to   35
pass her days in a sedan-chair.'

'Did you ever see her in it, uncle?' asked Mrs Joe.

'How could I,' he returned, forced to the admission, 'when I never see her in my life?   40
Never clapped eyes upon her!'

'Goodness, uncle! And yet you have spoken to her!'

'Why, don't you know,' said Mr Pumblechook testily, 'that when I have been there, I have been   45
took up to the outside of her door, and the door has stood ajar, and she has spoken to me that way. Don't say you don't know *that*, Mum. Howsever, the boy went there to play. What did you play at, boy?'   50

'We played with flags,' I said. (I beg to observe that I think of myself with amazement, when I recall the lies I told on this occasion.)

'Flags!' echoed my sister.

'Yes,' said I. 'Estella waved a blue flag, and I 55 waved a red one, and Miss Havisham waved one sprinkled all over with little gold stars, out at the coach-window. And then we all waved our swords and hurrahed.'

'Swords!' repeated my sister. 'Where did you 60 get swords from?'

'Out of a cupboard,' said I. 'And I saw pistols in it – and jam – and pills. And there was no daylight in the room, but it was all lighted up with candles.'

'That's true, Mum,' said Mr Pumblechook, 65 with a grave nod. 'That's the state of the case, for that much I've seen myself.' And then they both stared at me, and I, with an obtrusive show of artlessness on my countenance, stared at them, and plaited the right leg of my trousers with my 70 right hand.

From Chapter 9, pp. 96–98

---

1 Why does Pip comment to the reader 'as well they might' (line 7)?

2 Why do you think Pip feels 'reckless . . . under the torture' (line 22)?

3 Pip's lies – the velvet coach, gold plates, cake, wine, enormous dogs, silver baskets and veal cutlets, flags, swords – are all details from what sort of stories?

4 What is funny about Pip's story about the contents of the cupboard?

5 Why do you think Pip tells these lies?

Later that same day, Pip confides in Joe.

After Mr Pumblechook had driven off, and when my sister was washing up, I stole into the forge to Joe, and remained by him until he had done for the night. Then I said, 'Before the fire goes out, Joe, I should like to tell 5 you something.'

'Should you, Pip?' said Joe, drawing his shoeing-stool near the forge. 'Then tell us. What is it, Pip?'

'Joe,' said I, taking hold of his rolled-up shirt 10 sleeve, and twisting it between my finger and thumb, 'you remember all that about Miss Havisham's?'

'Remember?' said Joe. 'I believe you! Wonderful!' 15

'It's a terrible thing, Joe; it ain't true.'

'What are you telling of, Pip?' cried Joe, falling back in the greatest amazement. 'You don't mean to say it's—'

'Yes, I do; it's lies, Joe.' 20

'But not all of it? Why sure you don't mean to say, Pip, that there was no black welwet co—ch?' For I stood shaking my head. 'But at least there was dogs, Pip? Come, Pip,' said Joe, persuasively, 'if there warn't no weal-cutlets, at least there was 25 dogs?'

'No, Joe.'

'A dog?' said Joe, 'A puppy? Come!'

'No, Joe, there was nothing at all of the kind.'

As I fixed my eyes hopelessly on Joe, Joe 30 contemplated me in dismay. 'Pip, old chap! This won't do, old fellow! I say! Where do you expect to go to?'

'It's terrible, Joe; ain't it?'

'Terrible?' cried Joe. 'Awful! What possessed 35 you?'

'I don't know what possessed me, Joe,' I replied, letting his shirt sleeve go, and sitting down in the ashes at his feet, hanging my head; 'but I wish you hadn't taught me to call Knaves at 40 cards, Jacks; and I wish my boots weren't so thick nor my hands so coarse.'

And then I told Joe that I felt very miserable, and that I hadn't been able to explain myself to Mrs Joe and Pumblechook, who were so rude to 45 me, and that there had been a beautiful young lady at Miss Havisham's who was dreadfully proud, and that she had said I was common, and that I knew I was common, and that I wished I was not common, and that the lies had come of it 50 somehow, though I didn't know how.

This was a case of metaphysics, at least as difficult for Joe to deal with, as for me. But Joe took the case altogether out of the region of metaphysics, and by that means vanquished it. 55

'There's one thing you may be sure of, Pip,' said Joe, after some rumination, 'namely, that lies is lies. Howsever they come, they didn't ought to come, and they come from the father of lies, and work round to the same. Don't you tell no more of 60 'em, Pip. *That* ain't the way to get out of being common, old chap. And as to being common, I don't make it out at all clear. You are oncommon in some things. You're oncommon small. Likewise you're a oncommon scholar.' 65

'No, I am ignorant and backward, Joe.'

From Chapter 9, pp. 99–100

1 Why do you think Pip takes hold of Joe's rolled-up shirt sleeve, 'twisting it between my finger and thumb' (lines 11–12)?

2 What do you make of Joe from his reaction to Pip's confession (lines 30–36)?

3 What does Pip feel about himself (lines 49–50)? What might these feelings have to do with his wanting to tell lies about his visit to Miss Havisham's?

4 Is Joe being funny when he tells Pip, 'You are oncommon in some things. You're oncommon small. Likewise you're a oncommon scholar.' (lines 63–65)?

5 Why do you think Pip is so affected by Estella's calling him 'common'? Do you think it would be equally hurtful nowadays?

weeping willow at a tomb with an urn on it. I noticed, too, that several rings and seals hung at his watch-chain, as if he were quite laden with remembrances of departed friends. He had glittering eyes – small, keen, and black – and thin wide mottled lips. He had had them, to the best of my belief, from forty to fifty years. . . .

He wore his hat on the back of his head, and looked straight before him: walking in a self-contained way as if there were nothing in the streets to claim his attention. His mouth was such a post-office of a mouth that he had a mechanical appearance of smiling. We had got to the top of Holborn Hill before I knew that it was merely a mechanical appearance, and that he was not smiling at all.

From Chapter 21, pp. 195–196

MISS HAVISHAM AND PIP

Pip lies about his outing to Miss Havisham's house. What genuine feelings do you think he would have carried away with him but might have been unable to express? What might he have written in his diary or told to a close friend?

Pip meets Mr Wemmick (From the 1947 film *Great Expectations*)

Later on in the story, Pip unexpectedly receives a lot of money and is thus able to become a 'gentleman'. The money comes from a secret, unknown donor who gives Pip his allowance through a lawyer, Mr Jaggers. Pip comes to London where he meets Jaggers's clerk, Wemmick.

Casting my eyes on Mr Wemmick as we went along, to see what he was like in the light of day, I found him to be a dry man, rather short in stature, with a square wooden face, whose expression seemed to have been imperfectly chipped out with a dull-edged chisel. There were some marks in it that might have been dimples, if the material had been softer and the instrument finer, but which, as it was, were only dints. The chisel had made three or four of these attempts at embellishment over his nose, but had given them up without an effort to smooth them off. I judged him to be a bachelor from the frayed condition of his linen, and he appeared to have sustained a good many bereavements; for he wore at least four mourning rings, besides a brooch representing a lady and a

(You will have to read the book to find out later in the story where all the rings and brooches come from!)

1 What does Pip's description (lines 4–6) suggest about Wemmick's face?
2 Why might Pip notice Wemmick's way of walking (lines 26–28)?
3 What do you think is meant by 'a post-office of a mouth' (line 29)?

Pip soon finds that he has to deal with Mr Jaggers himself, when he decides to buy some furniture and needs some extra money. Jaggers's manner rather takes Pip aback.

I went off to Little Britain and imparted my wish to Mr Jaggers.

'If I could buy the furniture now hired for me,' said I, 'and one or two other little things, I should be quite at home there.'   5

'Go it!' said Mr Jaggers, with a short laugh. 'I told you you'd get on. Well! How much do you want?'

I said I didn't know how much.

'Come!' retorted Mr Jaggers. 'How much?   10
Fifty pounds?'

'Oh, not nearly so much.'

'Five pounds?' said Mr Jaggers.

This was such a great fall, that I said in discomfiture, 'Oh! more than that.'   15

'More than that, eh!' retorted Mr Jaggers, lying in wait for me, with his hands in his pockets, his head on one side, and his eyes on the wall behind me; 'how much more?'

'It is so difficult to fix a sum,' said I, hesitating. 20

'Come!' said Mr Jaggers. 'Let's get at it. Twice five; will that do? Three times five; will that do? Four times five; will that do?'

I said I thought that would do handsomely.

'Four times five will do handsomely, will it?' 25
said Mr Jaggers, knitting his brows. 'Now, what do you make of four times five?'

'What do I make of it?'

'Ah!' said Mr Jaggers; 'how much?'

'I suppose you make it twenty pounds,' said I, 30
smiling.

'Never mind what *I* make it, my friend,' observed Mr Jaggers, with a knowing and contradictory toss of the head. 'I want to know what *you* make it?'   35

'Twenty pounds, of course.'

'Wemmick!' said Mr Jaggers, opening his office door. 'Take Mr Pip's written order, and pay him twenty pounds.'

This strongly marked way of doing business   40
made a strongly marked impression on me, and that not of an agreeable kind. Mr Jaggers never laughed; but he wore great bright creaking boots; and, in poising himself on those boots, with his large head bent down and his eyebrows joined   45
together, awaiting an answer, he sometimes caused the boots to creak, as if *they* laughed in a dry and suspicious way. As he happened to go out now, and as Wemmick was brisk and talkative, I said to Wemmick that I hardly knew what to make   50
of Mr Jaggers's manner.

'Tell him that, and he'll take it as a compliment,' answered Wemmick; 'he don't mean that you *should* know what to make of it.—Oh!' for I looked surprised, 'it's not personal; it's profes-   55
sional: only professional.'

Wemmick was at his desk, lunching – and crunching – on a dry hard biscuit; pieces of which he threw from time to time into his slit of a mouth, as if he were posting them.   60

'Always seems to me,' said Wemmick, 'as if he had set a man-trap and was watching it. Suddenly – click – you're caught!'

Without remarking that man-traps were not among the amenities of life, I said I supposed he   65
was very skilful?

'Deep,' said Wemmick, 'as Australia.' Pointing with his pen at the office floor, to express that Australia was understood, for the purposes of the figure, to be symmetrically on the opposite spot of   70
the globe. 'If there was anything deeper,' added Wemmick, bringing his pen to paper, 'he'd be it.'

From Chapter 24, pp. 220–222

Pip negotiates with
Mr Jaggers
(From the 1947 film
Great Expectations)

Joe visits Pip in London (From the 1947 film *Great Expectations*)

1 How would you describe Jaggers's way of treating Pip (lines 10–39)?
2 Why does Pip say that the impression Mr Jaggers's style made on him was 'not of an agreeable kind' (line 42)?
3 Why might Pip think the creaking of the boots was a type of 'dry and suspicious' laughter (lines 46–48)?
4 What does 'posting' (line 60) bring to the reader's mind?
5 What does Wemmick mean by as 'deep as Australia' (line 67)?

Pip, in his dealings with Jaggers, notices a number of personal traits. One was how, as Pip put it, 'he washed his clients off'.

. . . he washed his clients off, as if it were a surgeon or a dentist. He had a closet in his room, fitted up for the purpose, which smelt of the scented soap like a perfumer's shop. It had an unusually large jack-towel on a roller inside the 5 door, and he would wash his hands and wipe them and dry them all over this towel, whenever he came in from a police-court or dismissed a client from his room. When I and my friends repaired to him at six o'clock next day, he seemed 10 to have been engaged on a case of a darker complexion than usual, for we found him with his head butted into this closet, not only washing his hands, but laving his face and gargling his throat. And even when he had done all that, and had 15 gone all round the jack-towel, he took out his penknife and scraped the case out of his nails before he put his coat on.

From Chapter 26, p. 233

1 Why might a lawyer such as Jaggers wash in this manner (lines 1–2)?
2 What is meant by 'a case of a darker complexion than usual' (lines 11–12)?
3 What does Pip mean by 'scraped the case out of his nails' (line 17)?

Pip starts to lead the life of a 'gentleman', receiving money from Mr Jaggers and learning how to behave and dress. After a short while he receives a visit from Joe, who has got dressed up for the occasion and is on his very best behaviour. Pip, who is still very fond of Joe, nonetheless is embarrassed by this visit from one of his humble relatives. The visit is not a success: Joe is very tense, and does not know what to do with his hat, and keeps calling Pip 'Sir'. Joe decides to cut the trip short. Pip is disappointed.

'**B**ut you are not going now, Joe?'

'Yes, I am,' said Joe.

'But you are coming back to dinner, Joe?'

'No I am not,' said Joe.   5

Our eyes met, and all the 'Sir' melted out of that manly heart as he gave me his hand.

'Pip, dear old chap, life is made of ever so many partings welded together, as I may say, and one man's a blacksmith, and one's a whitesmith, and 10 one's a goldsmith, and one's a coppersmith. Diwisions among such must come, and must be met as they come . If there's been any fault at all today, it's mine. You and me is not two figures to be together in London; nor yet anywheres else 15 but what is private, and beknown, and understood among friends. It ain't that I am proud, but that I want to be right, as you shall never see me no more in these clothes. I'm wrong in these clothes. I'm wrong out of the forge, the kitchen, 20 or off th' meshes. You won't find half so much fault in me if you think of me in my forge dress, with my hammer in my hand, or even my pipe. You won't find half so much fault in me if, supposing as you should ever wish to see me, you 25 come and put your head in at the forge window and see Joe the blacksmith, there, at the old anvil, in the old burnt apron, sticking to the old work. I'm awful dull, but I hope I've beat out something nigh the rights of this at last. And so GOD bless 30 you, dear old Pip, old chap, GOD bless you!'

From Chapter 27, p. 246

---

1 Why does Joe think they can't be together in London (lines 14–15)?

2 What does Joe mean by 'I'm wrong in these clothes' (lines 19–20)?

3 What is Joe trying to explain to Pip (lines 24–28)?

Great Expectations is a novel about a boy from a blacksmith's shop who is provoked into wanting to be a gentleman and who quite unexpectedly becomes one. Dickens focuses his full attention, and ours, on the related issues of social class and personal ambition. Miss Havisham, Estella, Joe, Jaggers, Wemmick and the convict all combine in an intriguing and powerful story written with great skill and humour as if through the ever-opening eyes of the narrator, Pip. It is a wonderful book – read it soon!

4

Dickens, man of the theatre

Throughout his life Dickens had a passion for the theatre. He loved to visit all kinds of theatres, was a keen amateur actor and director and, once he had become a world-famous novelist, he developed his own form of theatrical entertainment: the dramatic reading.

Grimaldi, the clown, performed regularly at Drury Lane and Sadler's Wells Theatre in the early nineteenth century

The popular theatre

As a young Londoner, working as a clerk in a solicitor's office and then as a reporter, he spent as many evenings as he could at the theatre. He entertained his fellow-clerks with his impersonations of famous actors, and also with his imitations of the office cleaning woman.

When he became a court reporter he began to think seriously about becoming an actor. He learnt parts by heart and wrote to the theatre manager at Covent Garden asking for an audition. He was granted one, but when the day came he had a bad cold and his face was swollen with toothache. He decided to re-apply for the next season and stayed away from his appointment. However, by the time the next round of auditions came up, Dickens was having some success as a journalist and he decided to keep working as a writer.

Later in his life, when he was a famous writer, he told his friend John Forster this story of the missed audition, and added the comment, 'see how near I may have been to another sort of life.'

At that time, there were only three serious theatres in London: Drury Lane, Covent Garden and the Haymarket. There were, however, a huge number of minor theatres: music halls, private theatres, semi-circuses, suburban theatres, cabarets and suchlike. These were less serious, more popular and far cheaper than the major theatres (some were known as 'penny theatres'). Dickens loved the bright and brash atmosphere of these cheap theatres and we find him writing about them in his early journalism and novels.

PRIVATE THEATRES

A private theatre was a place where one went to act rather than to watch. The owner would advertise the play and sell the parts to stage-struck members of the public: the best parts cost the most. One of his *Sketches by Boz* is about these theatres.

'RICHARD THE THIRD.—DUKE OF GLO'STER, 2*l*.; EARL OF RICHMOND, 1*l*.; DUKE OF BUCKINGHAM, 15*s*.; CATESBY, 12*s*.; TRESSEL, 10*s*. 6*d*.; LORD STANLEY, 5*s*.; LORD MAYOR OF LONDON, 2*s*. 6*d*.'

Such are the written placards wafered up in the gentlemen's dressing-room, or the green-room (where there is any), at a private theatre; and such are the sums extracted from the shop-till, or overcharged in the office expenditure, by the donkeys who are prevailed upon to pay for permission to exhibit their lamentable ignorance and boobyism on the stage of a private theatre. This they do, in proportion to the scope afforded by the character for the display of their imbecility. For instance, the Duke of Glo'ster is well worth two pounds, because he has it all to himself; he must wear a real sword, and what is better still, he must draw it several times in the course of the piece. The soliloquies alone are well worth fifteen shillings; then there is the stabbing King Henry – decidedly cheap at three-and-sixpence, that's eighteen-and-sixpence; bullying the coffin-bearers – say eighteenpence, though its worth much more – that's a pound. Then the love scene with Lady Ann, and the bustle of the fourth act can't be dear at ten shillings more – that's only one pound ten, including the 'off with his head!' – which is sure to bring down the applause, and it is very easy to do— 'Orf with his ed' (very quick and loud;—then slow and sneeringly)—'So much for Bu-u-u-uckingham!'

From 'Private Theatres' in *Sketches by Boz*

Dickens goes on to describe more of the acting style popular at such theatres, and then turns his attention to the audience.

The principal patrons of private theatres are dirty boys, low copying-clerks in attorneys' offices, capacious-headed youths from city counting-houses, Jews whose business, as lenders of fancy dresses, is a sure passport to the amateur stage, shop-boys who now and then mistake their masters' money for their own; and a choice miscellany of idle vagabonds. The proprietor of a private theatre may be an ex-scene-painter, a low coffee-house-keeper, a disappointed eighth-rate actor, a retired smuggler, or uncertificated bankrupt. The theatre itself may be in Catherine Street, Strand, the purlieus of the city, the neighbourhood of Gray's Inn Lane, or the vicinity of Sadler's Wells; or it may, perhaps, form the chief nuisance of some shabby street, on the Surrey side of Waterloo Bridge.

The lady performers pay nothing for their characters, and it is needless to add, are usually selected from one class of society; the audiences are necessarily of much the same character as the performers, who receive, in return for their contributions to the management, tickets to the amount of the money they pay.

We gain an insight into why these theatres were popular when Dickens adds the following detail:

The two stout men in the centre box, with an opera-glass ostentatiously placed before them, are friends of the proprietor – opulent country managers, as he confidentially informs every individual among the crew behind the curtain – opulent country managers looking out for recruits; a representation which Mr Nathan, the dresser, who is in the manager's interest, and has just arrived with the costumes, offers to confirm upon oath if required – corroborative evidence, however, is quite unnecessary, for the gulls believe it at once.

FOR DISCUSSION

1 What is Dickens implying in his comment about the 'lady performers'?
2 What sort of fun would 'dirty boys' and 'low copying-clerks' have at such a theatre?

ASTLEY'S

Another very popular theatre in London at that time was Astley's: this was a theatre that would seem more of a circus to a modern theatre-goer. Melodramas with plenty of fighting were mixed in with performances by highly-trained and decorated horses. One of the *Sketches* concentrates on Astley's and it is also described in *The Old Curiosity Shop*, when the Nubbles family visit it on one of their rare nights out.

Astley's Royal
Amphitheatre

Dear, dear, what a place it looked, that Astley's! with all the paint, gilding, and looking-glass; the vague smell of horses suggestive of coming wonders; the curtain that hid such gorgeous mysteries; the clean white sawdust down in the circus, the company coming in and taking their places; the fiddlers looking carelessly up at them while they tuned their instruments, as if they didn't want the play to begin, and knew it all beforehand! What a glow was that which burst upon them all, when that long, clear, brilliant row of lights came slowly up; and what the feverish excitement when the little bell rang and the music began in good earnest; with strong parts for the drums, and sweet effects for the triangles! Well might Barbara's mother say to Kit's mother that the gallery was the place to see from, and wonder it wasn't much dearer than the boxes; and well might Barbara feel doubtful whether to laugh or cry, in her flutter of delight.

Then the play itself! the horses which little Jacob believed from the first to be alive, and the ladies and gentlemen of whose reality he could be by no means persuaded, having never seen or heard anything at all like them – the firing, which made Barbara wink – the forlorn lady, who made her cry – the tyrant, who made her tremble – the man who sung the song with the lady's-maid and danced the chorus, who made her laugh – the pony who reared up on his hind legs when he saw the murderer, and wouldn't hear of walking on all fours again until he was taken into custody – the clown who ventured on such familiarities with the military man in boots – the lady who jumped over the nine-and-twenty ribbons and came down safe upon the horse's back – everything was delightful, splendid, and surprising. Little Jacob applauded till his hands were sore; Kit cried 'an-kor' at the end of everything, the three-act piece included; and Barbara's mother beat her umbrella on the floor, in her ecstacies, until it was nearly worn down to the gingham.

From *The Old Curiosity Shop*, Ch. 39, p. 376

ACTIVITY

Design a poster advertising this event.

A TOURING COMPANY

The theatre is also the subject of a section of *Nicholas Nickleby*, when the hero and his friend Smike join a travelling theatre group, run by Mr Crummles. Nicholas and Smike are penniless and Nicholas is thinking of going to sea, when Mr Crummles makes another suggestion.

'Does no other profession occur to you, which a young man of your figure and address could take up easily, and see the world to advantage in?' asked the manager.

'No,' said Nicholas, shaking his head.

'Why, then, I'll tell you one,' said Mr Crummles, throwing his pipe into the fire, and raising his voice. 'The stage!'

'The stage!' cried Nicholas, in a voice almost as loud.

'The theatrical profession,' said Mr Vincent Crummles. 'I am in the theatrical profession myself, my wife is in the theatrical profession, my children are in the theatrical profession. I had a dog that lived and died in it from a puppy; and my chaise-pony goes on in Timour the Tartar. I'll bring you out, and your friend too. Say the word. I want a novelty.'

'I don't know anything about it,' rejoined Nicholas, whose breath had been almost taken away by this sudden proposal. 'I never acted a part in my life, except at school.'

'There's genteel comedy in your walk and manner, juvenile tragedy in your eye, and touch-and-go farce in your laugh,' said Mr Vincent Crummles. 'You'll do as well as if you had thought of nothing else but the lamps, from your birth downwards.'

Nicholas thought of the small amount of small change there would remain in his pocket after paying the tavern bill: and he hesitated.

'You can be useful to us in a hundred ways,' said Mr Crummles. 'Think what capital bills a man of your education could write for the shop-windows.'

'Well, I think I could manage that department,' said Nicholas.

'To be sure you could,' replied Mr Crummles. '"For further particulars see small hand-bills" – we might have half a volume in every one of them. Pieces too; why, you could write us a piece to bring out the whole strength of the company, whenever we wanted one.'

'I am not quite so confident about that,' replied Nicholas. 'But I dare say I could scribble something now and then that would suit you.'

'We'll have a new show-piece out directly,' said the manager. 'Let me see – peculiar resources of this establishment – new and splendid scenery – you must manage to introduce a real pump and two washing-tubs.'

'Into the piece?' said Nicholas.

'Yes,' replied the manager. 'I bought 'em cheap, at a sale the other day; and they'll come in admirably. That's the London plan. They look up some dresses, and properties, and have a piece written to fit them. Most of the theatres keep an author on purpose.'

'Indeed!' cried Nicholas.

'Oh yes,' said the manager; 'a common thing. It'll look very well in the bills in separate lines – Real pump! – Splendid tubs! – Great attraction! You don't happen to be anything of an artist, do you?'

'That is not one of my accomplishments,' rejoined Nicholas.

'Ah! Then it can't be helped,' said the manager. 'If you had been, we might have had a large woodcut of the last scene for the posters, showing the whole depth of the stage, with the pump and tubs in the middle; but however, if you're not, it can't be helped.'

'What should I get for all this?' inquired Nicholas, after a few moments' reflection. 'Could I live by it?'

'Live by it!' said the manager. 'Like a prince! With your own salary, and your friend's, and your writings, you'd make – ah! you'd make a pound a week!'

'You don't say so!'

'I do indeed, and if we had a run of good houses, nearly double the money.'

From *Nicholas Nickleby*, Ch. 22, pp. 359–60

WRITING

What do you think Nicholas would write? Write an extract from his play.

So Nicholas and Smike join Mr Crummles's troupe and continue their journey with him. On the way Mr Crummles tells Nicholas about the theatrical origins of their pony.

'He's a good pony at bottom,' said Mr Crummles, turning to Nicholas.

He might have been at bottom, but he certainly was not at top, seeing that his coat was of the roughest and most ill-favoured kind. So, Nicholas merely observed, that he shouldn't wonder if he was.

'Many and many is the circuit this pony has gone,' said Mr Crummles, flicking him skilfully on the eyelid for old acquaintance' sake. 'He is quite one of us. His mother was on the stage.'

'Was she, indeed?' rejoined Nicholas.

'She ate apple-pie at a circus for upwards of fourteen years,' said the manager; 'fired pistols, and went to bed in a nightcap; and, in short, took the low comdey entirely. His father was a dancer.'

'Was he at all distinguished?'

'Not very,' said the manager. 'He was rather a low sort of pony. The fact is, that he had been originally jobbed out by the day, and he never quite got over his old habits. He was clever in melodrama too, but too broad – too broad. When the mother died, he took the port-wine business.'

'The port-wine business!' cried Nicholas.

'Drinking port-wine with the clown,' said the manager, 'but he was greedy, and one night bit off the bowl of the glass, and choked himself, so that his vulgarity was the death of him at last.'

From *Nicholas Nickleby*, Ch. 23, pp. 361–2

FOR DISCUSSION

1 What do you think Mr Crummles means by 'took', as in 'took the low comedy entirely' and 'took the port-wine business'?

2 What do you think he means by the following phrases: 'a low sort of pony'; 'too broad'; 'his vulgarity'?

Twenty years later, in his novel *Hard Times* Dickens wrote about another travelling troupe – Mr Sleary's travelling circus. Dickens uses them to create a contrast between their warmth and generosity and the cold mean atmosphere of Coketown, the northern town they are visiting (see extract on page 39).

Meanwhile, the various members of Sleary's company gradually gathered together from the upper regions, where they were quartered, and, from standing about, talking in low voices to one another and to Mr Childers, gradually insinuated themselves . . . into the room. There were two or three handsome young women among them, with their two or three husbands, and their two or three mothers, and their eight or nine little children, who did the fairy business when required. The father of one of the families was in the habit of balancing the father of another of the families on the top of a great pole; the father of a third family often made a pyramid of both those fathers, with Master Kidderminster for the apex, and himself for the base; all the fathers could dance upon rolling casks, stand upon bottles, catch knives and balls, twirl hand-basins, ride upon anything, jump over everything and stick at nothing. All the mothers could – and did – dance upon the slack wire and the tight-rope, and perform rapid acts on bare-backed steeds; none of them were at all particular in respect of showing their legs; and one of them, alone in a Greek chariot, drove six-in-hand into every town they came to. They all assumed to be mighty rakish and knowing, they were not very tidy in their private dresses, they were not at all orderly in their domestic arrangements, and the combined literature of the whole company would have produced but a poor letter on any subject. Yet there was a remarkable gentleness and childishness about these people, a special inaptitude for any kind of sharp practice, and an untiring readiness to help and pity one another, deserving often of as much respect, and always of as much generous construction, as the every day virtues of any class of people in the world.

From *Hard Times*, Book the First, Ch. 6, p. 77

FOR DISCUSSION

1 What does Dickens note about these people that some of his readers might have found socially unacceptable?

2 What does Dickens suggest is special about these people?

DICKENS'S ATTITUDE TO THE POPULAR THEATRE

The popular theatre also features in another of Dickens's later novels. In *Great Expectations* the narrator Pip, and his friend, Herbert Pocket, go to see Mr Wopsle, an old acquaintance of Pip's, perform in *Hamlet*. Mr Wopsle has given up his respectable life in the little town where Pip grew up and has come to London to try his luck as an actor. Pip learns of Mr Wopsle's new career and takes his friend Herbert to see the play.

Dickens quickly establishes the atmosphere in the theatre.

O n our arrival in Denmark, we found the king and queen of that country elevated in two arm-chairs on a kitchen-table holding a Court. The whole of the Danish nobility were in attendance; consisting of a noble boy in the wash-leather boots of a gigantic ancestor, a venerable Peer with a dirty face, who seemed to have risen from the people late in life, and the Danish chivalry with a comb in its hair and a pair of white silk legs, and presenting on the whole a feminine appearance. My

gifted townsman stood gloomily apart, with folded arms, and I could have wished that his curls and forehead had been more probable.

The play progresses amid a good deal of heckling from the audience, much of it directed at Mr Wopsle, who is playing Hamlet himself.

O n his taking the recorders – very like a little black flute that had just been played in the orchestra and handed out at the door – he was called upon unanimously for Rule Britannia. When he recommended the player not to saw the air thus, the sulky man said, 'And don't *you* do it, neither; you're a deal worse than *him*!' And I grieve to add that peals of laughter greeted Mr Wopsle on every one of these occasions.

But his greatest trials were in the churchyard: which had the appearance of a primeval forest, with a kind of small ecclesiastical wash-house on one side, and a turnpike gate on the other. Mr Wopsle, in a comprehensive black cloak, being descried entering at the turnpike, the gravedigger was admonished in a friendly way, 'Look out! Here's the undertaker a coming, to see how you're getting on with your work!' I believe it is well known in a constitutional country that Mr Wopsle could not possibly have returned the skull, after moralising over it, without dusting his fingers on a white napkin taken from his breast; but even that innocent and indispensable action did not pass without the comment 'Wai-ter!'

From *Great Expectations*, Ch. 31, pp. 273–5

It is clear from this episode that Dickens found the atmosphere among the audience more involving than the semi-professional performances he saw at the minor theatres. But Dickens was very serious about the importance of the popular theatre, as we can see from the following piece, which he wrote for his own journal, *Household Words*.

T here is a range of imagination in most of us, which no amount of steam-engines will satisfy; and which The-great-exhibition-of-the-works-of-industry-of-all-nations, itself, will probably leave unappeased. The lower we go, the more natural it is that the best-relished provision for this should be found in dramatic entertainments; as at once the most obvious, the least troublesome, and the most real, of

The New Cut,
Lambeth, in the
early evening

all escapes out of the literal world. Joe Whelks, of the New Cut, Lambeth, is not much of a reader, has no great store of books, no very commodious room to read in, no very decided inclination to read, and no power at all of presenting vividly before his mind's eye what he reads about. But put Joe in the Gallery of the Victoria Theatre; show him doors and windows in the scene that will open and shut, and that people can get in and out of; tell him a story with these aids, and by the help of live men and women dressed up, confiding to him their innermost secrets, in voices audible half a mile off; and Joe will unravel a story through all its entanglements, and sit there as long after midnight as you have anything left to show him. Accordingly, the Theatres to which Mr Whelks resorts are always full; and whatever changes of fashion the drama knows elsewhere, it is always fashionable in the New Cut.

From 'The Amusements of the People –I'
Household Words, 30 March 1850

This is a very serious point: steam-engines and other 'scientific' exhibitions were seen to be educational, but the popular theatre was not. Dickens is here recognising the importance of such theatres to a semi-literate and illiterate audience.

In a follow-up to this article Dickens extends his argument and points out other advantages of well-run popular theatres, such as the Eagle in the City Road. He writes about the way such theatres put the interests of ordinary people first and how this is clear from the seating arrangements as much as from anything else.

Instead of being at a great disadvantage in comparison with the mass of the audience, they were *the* audience, for whose accommodation the place was made. We believe this to be one great cause of the success of these speculations. In whatever way the common people are addressed, whether in churches, chapels, schools, lecture-rooms, or theatres, to be successfully addressed they must be directly appealed to. No matter how good the feast, they will not come to it on mere sufferance. If, on looking round us, we find that the only things plainly and personally addressed to them, from quack medicines upwards, be bad or very defective things, – so much the worse for them and for all of us, and so much the more unjust and absurd the system which has haughtily abandoned a strong ground to such occupation.

We will add that we believe these people have a right to be amused. A great deal that we consider to be unreasonable is written and talked about not licensing these places of entertainment.

From 'The Amusements of the People – II'
Household Words, 6 April 1850

Dickens's own contribution to the theatre has been indirect. His own plays – many of them short farces written when a young man – are undistinguished and really only of curiosity value. He did not write any major works for the stage. However, stage-versions of his books appeared almost as soon as they were published, and they continue to be adapted for television, films, musicals, radio and the theatre. In recent years the Royal Shakespeare Company made theatre history with their production of *Nicholas Nickleby*. It was staged in two parts, was nearly nine hours long, and was an enormous success. It held audiences spellbound in London and New York and was eventually recorded for television.

More recently, Christine Edzard's masterly two-part film of *Little Dorrit* (Sands Films, London 1987) has been capturing the imagination of cinema audiences.

FOR DISCUSSION

Imagine Dickens's ghost spent a week watching modern television: which three programmes do you think he would like most?

WRITING

Dickens's ghost visits your home and spends an evening watching television with you. He then writes up the experience in the article for *Household Words*. Write the article.

The accomplished amateur

'I had been a writer when I was a mere baby, and always an actor from the same age.'

Dickens wrote these lines to his friend the novelist Wilkie Collins in 1856. His nurse Mary Weller recalled how, as a young child, Dickens had delighted in performing songs and reciting poems in front of other members of the family. He also appeared in plays at school and enjoyed visiting the theatre from a very young age. He loved clowns and clowning, but was also impressed by cheap productions of Shakespeare that he saw. We have seen how, as a young man, he enjoyed visiting London's theatres and how close he came to becoming an actor.

By 1842 Dickens was an established writer of international fame. He took a trip to the United States and Canada, and it was while he was in Montreal that we find him putting on his first amateur production. He directed a troupe of army officers and their wives in three comic plays for one night only. It was a private performance and admission was by invitation. As Dickens wrote to his friend Forster, a journalist and author:

The pains I have taken with them (the other 'actors'), and the perspiration I have expended, during the last ten days, exceed in amount anything you can imagine. I had regular plots of scenery made out, and lists of the properties wanted; and had them nailed up by the prompter's chair. Every letter that was to be delivered was written; every piece of money that had to be given, provided; and not a single thing lost sight of. I prompted, myself, when I was not on; when I was, I made the regular prompter of the theatre my deputy . . .

Quoted in John Forster's *Life of Charles Dickens*, III, Chapter 7

This was to be Dickens's major relaxation, on and off, for the next fifteen years, and the pattern of productions remained remarkably similar to this first one: a small group of friends, working under Dickens's meticulous direction and management, and staging, at first, private performances. These productions became so famous that Dickens was quick to realise that they could be staged as public performances in order to raise money for charity.

Right:
A programme for *Every Man in His Humour*, with drawings by Daniel Maclise of John Forster (as Kitely) and Dickens (as Captain Bobadil)

Left:
Dickens as Bobadil in *Every Man in His Humour*

scene arranger, property-man, prompter, and bandmaster. Without offending anyone he kept everyone in order...' (Forster, *Life of Charles Dickens*, V, Ch. 1)

The first production in this country was during the autumn of 1845, when Dickens and a team of amateurs, which included most of the staff of the newly-established *Punch* magazine, put on a production of Ben Jonson's *Every Man in His Humour*. The performance was at a private theatre in Soho on 21 September 1845. It was so successful that the cast was persuaded to put on a charity performance soon afterwards. The same cast did another production at the same theatre later in 1845, this time of *The Elder Brother* by Beaumont and Fletcher.

Dickens was a big success as an actor, particularly as Bobadil in *Every Man in His Humour*. He also impressed the cast with his energy as 'the stage-director, very often the stage carpenter,

DICKENS'S AMATEUR PRODUCTIONS

1845   *Every Man in His Humour*
       The Elder Brother

1847   Revival of *Every Man in His Humour*: company travelled by rail to Manchester and Liverpool. Performances given as benefits for Leigh Hunt, a poet and journalist.

1848   *Merry Wives of Windsor*: London performance attended by Queen Victoria and Prince Albert. Company went on to perform in Manchester, Liverpool, Edinburgh, Birmingham and Glasgow.

1850   Revival of *Merry Wives of Windsor*. Idea developed of setting up a permanent charity for writers and artists.

1851   New play, *Not so Bad as We Seem*, written for the new charity by Bulwer Lytton and performed before a society audience including the Queen and Prince Albert. Followed by a public tour.

An amateur performance of Bulwer Lytton's new comedy, *Not So Bad as We Seem*, before Queen Victoria and Prince Albert at Devonshire House, London

1854 Dickens set up 'The Smallest Theatre in the World' in his own house in London. Christmas plays performed by Dickens and Mark Lemon (editor of *Punch*) and the children from both families.

1855 Performance of Wilkie Collins's play *The Lighthouse* in the Smallest Theatre.

1856 Another new play by Collins, *The Frozen Deep*, first performed in the Smallest Theatre.

1857 Touring production of *The Frozen Deep* to raise money for the family of Douglas Jerrold, who had died suddenly. Performances staged in London and Manchester. Professional actresses employed to play female roles. Thus Dickens met and fell in love with Ellen Ternan, a young actress.

OPINIONS OF DICKENS AS AN ACTOR

'Had he, as he was once minded to, taken up acting as a profession he would have been as famous as Garrick.'

Lord Redesdale, diplomat and author

'If that man would go upon the stage, he would make his £10,000 a year!'

W. M. Thackeray, author, after seeing Dickens in *The Frozen Deep*.

'Ah, Mr Dickens, it was a sad loss to the public when you took to writing.'

Stage Carpenter, Haymarket Theatre, London.

Dickens's years as an amateur actor made him realise two things: the first was that he loved performing. He told Mary Cowden Clark, a journalist and member of his amateur company, 'There's nothing in the world equal to seeing the house rise at you, one sea of delighted faces, one hurrah of applause!' The second, equally important, thing was that he realised that he could earn a very good living as a performer. But what sort of performer might he, the world-famous author, speechmaker, journalist and editor, become?

The public reader

The answer to the question was easily found. The idea had been with him for years. In 1846 he had first, half-jokingly, suggested in a letter to Forster that he could make a good living giving public readings from his own books. However, both men had considered it rather beneath a great writer's dignity.

In 1853, however, he gave his first public reading at Birmingham Town Hall, where he read *A Christmas Carol*, followed two days later by *The Cricket on the Hearth*. These were both given in order to raise money for the Birmingham Institute, a centre for adult education. This gave rise to a number of readings, all for charity, over the next few years.

After meeting Ellen Ternan, in 1857, Dickens found himself, by the spring of 1858, in a state of great emotional turmoil. His marriage was breaking down and he was not working on a novel, nor was he involved in any 'theatricals'. From all over the country organisations were writing to him asking him to give readings and offering good fees. The temptation was clearly enormous. Here was something that would put him in front of a loving audience, that could earn him a lot of money and that would involve him totally as an author, actor and, as proved to be the case, editor of his own works. It would also get him away from the emotional and financial tangles he was in. He was in the process of buying Gad's Hill Place in Kent, and if he *was* going to separate from his wife he would need income to pay for the new house and for her maintenance. He wrote to Forster:

> . . . My determination is all but taken. I must do *Something*, or I shall wear my heart away. I can see no better thing to do that is half so hopeful in itself, or half so well suited to my restless state.

And restless he certainly was. He gave his first paid reading on 29 April 1858 and by the middle of May had separated from his wife. So Dickens's decision to become a Public Reader was a major life decision. It launched him on a new and highly profitable career and was entangled with his decision to leave his wife. This separation also provoked a bitter quarrel with his old friend Mark Lemon, editor of *Punch* and one of the key figures in the amateur theatricals that had involved them both since 1845. The old group of regular collaborators never met again.

Right:
Ellen Ternan and her sisters, Maria and Frances, whose association with the author began with the Manchester performances of *The Frozen Deep*

Far right:
Gad's Hill Place, with Dickens in the foreground

FACTS ABOUT THE PUBLIC READINGS

Total number of readings given:	472
Total earnings:	About £45,000
Most successful tour:	America – December 1867 to April 1868; 75 readings given
Earnings in America:	Nearly £20,000
Earnings per reading in 1858:	£40 (as much as the country's leading actor Macready earned for a performance)
Audiences:	Often over 2000

Effects of public readings:

- Enormous popularity
- Very high earnings
- Dickens's health broken by demands of touring and exhaustion from performing

Countries visited: England, Scotland, Ireland, USA

Most frequent items:

- The Trial from *Pickwick*
- *A Christmas Carol*
- Boots at the Holly Tree Inn
- Doctor Marigold
- *David Copperfield*
- Mr Bob Sawyer's Party
- Mrs Gamp

Most dramatic reading: Sikes and Nancy

OPINIONS OF DICKENS AS A PUBLIC READER

'Sikes and Nancy . . . it's two Macbeths!'

W. C. Macready, actor.

'Dickens acts better than any Macready in the world; a whole tragic, comic, heroic **theatre** visible, performing under one **hat** and keeping us laughing – in a very sorry way some of us thought – the whole night.'

Thomas Carlyle, author.

'A day or two before he died, I am told on good authority, he was found in the grounds of Gad's Hill, acting the murder scene between Sikes and Nancy.'

John Hollingshead, journalist.

'Attending his Readings, character after character appeared before us, living and breathing, in the flesh, as we looked and listened. It mattered nothing, just simply nothing, that the great author was there all the while before his audience in his own identity. His evening costume was a matter of no consideration – the flower in his button-hole, the paper-knife in his hand, the book before him, that earnest, animated, mobile, delightful face, that we all knew by heart through his ubiquitous photographs – all were equally of no account whatever. We knew that he alone was there all the time before us, reading, or, to speak more accurately, recreating for us, one and all – while his lips were articulating the familiar words his hand had written so many years previously – the most renowned of the imaginary creatures peopling his books. Watching him, hearkening to him, while he stood there unmistakably before his audience, on the raised platform, in the glare of the gas-burners shining down upon him from behind the pendant screen immediately above his head, his individual-

Dickens the public reader

ity, so to express it, altogether disappeared, and we saw before us instead, just as the case might happen to be, Mr Pickwick, or Mrs Gamp, or Dr Marigold, or little Paul Dombey, or Mr Squeers, or Sam Weller, or Mr Peggotty, or some other of those immortal personages . . .

'The way in which he threw himself into his labours, as a Reader, was only another indication of his intense affection for the dramatic art. For, as we have already insisted, the Readings were more than simply Readings, they were in the fullest meaning of the words singularly ingenious and highly elaborated histrionic performances.'

Charles Kent, journalist.

There is a great deal of evidence to support the idea that Dickens hastened his own death by exhausting himself giving the public readings. Towards the end of his life Dickens confessed that it had been 'madness' to perform the Sikes and Nancy reading so often. He had already given up reading once, in 1861, because it exhausted him so much, but had returned to it and earned enormous amounts, particularly in America.

It is clear from the accounts we have read that the readings used all of Dickens's acting skills. We can also see, from the existing copies of the texts he read, how carefully he *edited* each piece so that it read aloud as a self-contained dramatic item. The success of the readings was built upon two more points: the first is that Dickens's writing is essentially dramatic, in that the conversations are as good as any playwright's dialogue. The second point is that Dickens was a 'star' or, as Mary Cowden Clark described him, he was the public's 'literary idol'. He was immensely popular as a writer and this alone would have packed houses for his readings and amateur productions.

In giving the readings, Dickens's fame and popularity combined with the dramatic qualities of his writing, enhanced by his acting and editing skills. All this produced an intensely powerful theatrical experience that left audiences spell-bound and the reader exhausted.

Dickens did not invent the public reading as a form of entertainment, but he raised the state of the art to new-found heights. As Carlyle said, it was a whole theatre 'performing under one hat'. Dickens the Reader was not simply a man *of* the theatre: he *was* a theatre!

ACTIVITY

Using the extract given below (or one you have found yourself) prepare a 'reading'. This can be a solo performance, like Dickens's own, or it can be done by a small group, each reader taking specific parts plus a narrator. If you choose your own extract, select one that includes a fair amount of conversation. If you are working on a particular book as a class, try selecting a number of extracts from the book, arrange them for group readings and then compile your readings on a tape.

Whether you are working alone, as a group or as a class, you will soon discover how well Dickens's writing adapts to being read aloud.

FOR READING ALOUD

'Pip's Christmas Dinner' from *Great Expectations*, Chapter 4.

Pip, the narrator (story-teller) of the novel, describes a Christmas dinner from his childhood. He is an orphan and has been brought up by his bad-tempered sister and her gentle husband Joe, the village blacksmith.

I opened the door to the company – making believe that it was a habit of ours to open that door – and I opened it first to Mr Wopsle, next to Mr and Mrs Hubble, and last of all to Uncle Pumblechook. N.B. *I* was not allowed to call him uncle, under the severest penalties.

'Mrs Joe,' said Uncle Pumblechook; a large hard-breathing middle-aged slow man, with a mouth like a fish, dull staring eyes, and sandy hair standing upright on his head, so that he looked as if he had just been all but choked, and had that moment come to; 'I have brought you as the compliments of the season – I have brought you, Mum, a bottle of sherry wine – and I have brought you, Mum, a bottle of port wine.'

Every Christmas Day he presented himself, as a profound novelty, with exactly the same words, and carrying the two bottles like dumb-bells. Every Christmas Day, Mrs Joe replied, as she now replied, 'Oh, Un—cle Pum—ble—chook! This is kind!' Every Christmas Day, he retorted, as he now retorted, 'It's no more than your merits. And now are you all bobbish, and how's Sixpennorth of halfpence?' meaning me.

We dined on these occasions in the kitchen, and adjourned, for the nuts and oranges and apples, to the parlour; which was a change very like Joe's change from his working clothes to his Sunday dress. My sister was uncommonly lively on the present occasion, and indeed was generally more gracious in the society of Mrs Hubble than in other company. I remember Mrs Hubble as a little curly sharp-edged person in sky-blue, who held a conventionally juvenile position, because she had married Mr Hubble – I don't know at what remote period – when she was much younger than he. I remember Mr Hubble as a tough high-shouldered stooping old man, of a sawdusty fragance, with his legs extraordinarily wide apart: so that in my short days I always saw some miles of open country between them when I met him coming up the lane.

Among this good company I should have felt myself, even if I hadn't robbed the pantry, in a false position. Not because I was squeezed in at an acute angle of the table-cloth, with the table in my chest, and the Pumblechookian elbow in my eye, nor because I was not allowed to speak (I didn't want to speak), nor because I was regaled with the scaly tips of the drumsticks of the fowls, and with those obscure corners of pork of which the pig, when living, had had the least reason to be vain. No; I should not have minded that if they would only have left me alone. But they wouldn't leave me alone. They seemed to think the opportunity lost, if they failed to point the conversation at me, every now and then, and stick the point into me. I might have been an unfortunate little bull in a Spanish arena, I got so smartingly touched up by these moral goads.

It began the moment we sat down to dinner. Mr Wopsle said grace with theatrical declamation – as it now appears to me, something like a religious cross of the Ghost in Hamlet with Richard the Third – and ended with the very proper aspiration that we might be truly grateful. Upon which my sister fixed me with her eye, and said, in a low reproachful voice, 'Do you hear that? Be grateful.'

'Especially,' said Mr Pumblechook, 'be grateful, boy, to them which brought you up by hand.'

Mrs Hubble shook her head, and contemplating me with a mournful presentiment that I should come to no good, asked, 'Why is it that the young are never grateful?' This moral mystery seemed too much for the company until Mr Hubble tersely solved it by saying, 'Naterally wicious.' Everybody then murmured 'True!' and looked at me in a particularly unpleasant and personal manner.

Joe's station and influence were something feebler (if possible) when there was company, than when there was none. But he always aided and comforted me when he could, in some way of his own, and he always did so at dinner-time by giving me gravy, if there were any. There being plenty of gravy today, Joe spooned into my plate, at this point, about half a pint.

A little later on in the dinner, Mr Wopsle reviewed the sermon with some severity, and intimated – in the usual hypothetical case of the Church being 'thrown open' – what kind of a sermon *he* would have given them. After favouring them with some heads of that discourse, he remarked that he considered the subject of the day's homily, ill-chosen; which was the less excusable, he added, when there were so many subjects 'going about.'

'True again,' said Uncle Pumblechook. 'You've hit it, sir! Plenty of subjects going about, for them that know how to put salt upon their tails. That's what's wanted. A man needn't go far to find a subject, if he's ready with his salt-box.' Mr Pumblechook added, after a short interval of reflection, 'Look at Pork alone. There's a subject! If you want a subject, look at Pork!'

'True, sir. Many a moral for the young,' returned Mr Wopsle; and I knew he was going to lug me in, before he said it; 'might be deduced from that text.'

('You listen to this,' said my sister to me, in a severe parenthesis.)

Joe gave me some more gravy.

'Swine,' pursued Mr Wopsle, in his deepest voice, and pointing his fork at my blushes, as if he were mentioning my christian name; 'Swine were the companions of the prodigal. The gluttony of Swine is put before us, as an example to the young.' (I thought this pretty well in him who had been praising up the pork for being so plump and juicy.) 'What is detestable in a pig, is more detestable in a boy.'

'Or girl,' suggested Mr Hubble.

'Of course, or girl, Mr Hubble,' assented Mr Wopsle, rather irritably, 'but there is no girl present.'

'Besides,' said Mr Pumblechook, turning sharp on me, 'think what you've got to be grateful for. If you'd been born a Squeaker—'

'He *was*, if ever a child was,' said my sister, most emphatically.

Joe gave me some more gravy.

'Well, but I mean a four-footed Squeaker,' said Mr Pumblechook. 'If you had been born such, would you have been here now? Not you—'

'Unless in that form,' said Mr Wopsle, nodding towards the dish.

'But I don't mean in that form, sir,' returned Mr Pumblechook, who had an objection to being interrupted; 'I mean, enjoying himself with his elders and betters, and improving himself with their conversation, and rolling in the lap of luxury. Would he have been doing that? No, he wouldn't. And what would have been your destination?' turning on me again. 'You would have been disposed of for so many shillings according to the market price of the article, and Dunstable the butcher would have come up to you as you lay in your straw, and he would have whipped you under his left arm, and with his right he would have tucked up his frock to get a penknife from out of his waistcoat-pocket, and he would have shed your blood and had your life. No bringing up by hand then. Not a bit of it!'

Joe offered me more gravy, which I was afraid to take.

'He was a world of trouble to you, ma'am,' said Mrs Hubble, commiserating my sister.

'Trouble?' echoed my sister, 'trouble?' And then entered on a fearful catalogue of all the illnesses I had been guilty of, and all the acts of sleeplessness I had committed, and all the high places I had tumbled from, and all the low places I had tumbled into, and all the injuries I had done myself, and all the times she had wished me in my grave, and I had contumaciously refused to go there.

From *Great Expectations*, Ch. 4

5

Dickens the public figure

Dickens's fame as a novelist made him a public figure. His opinions on public issues became known not only through his novels, but from his additional work as a speechmaker, journalist, editor and campaigner. He wrote articles for newspapers and journals on issues about which he felt strongly. In 1846 he set up and had a very brief spell as editor of a daily newspaper, the *Daily News*, and in 1850 he set up his own journal, *Household Words*. In 1858 he reprinted some of his own pieces written for the journal, and published them in book form as *Reprinted Pieces*. In the following year, as a result of wrangles with his publisher, he closed down *Household Words* and set up a new journal, *All The Year Round*. After a few years he republished some of his own work

from this journal, and called the collection *The Uncommercial Traveller*. This book first appeared in 1861 and later editions were published with new pieces added in.

The two books, *Reprinted Pieces* and *The Uncommercial Traveller*, are widely available. Some of the pieces written by Dickens but not republished in these collections are harder to get hold of (see *Select bibliography* at the end of this book).

Below:
Dickens agreed with his publishers to the founding of a new daily newspaper, the *Daily News*

Above right:
Baroness Burdett-Coutts

Poverty

We have seen how poverty, particularly urban poverty, became a major social and political issue in the nineteenth century. The New Poor Law set up workhouses all over the country and yet the system failed to meet the needs of the poor. On 26 January 1856, Dickens's cover story for that week's issue of *Household Words* concerned the scene he had witnessed outside a London workhouse where destitute people queued for several nights to gain admission.

A NIGHTLY SCENE IN LONDON

Dickens was much in demand as a speaker, particularly at charity dinners, where money would be raised and several speeches given by celebrities. Dickens spoke at many such dinners, raising money for schools, hospitals and charitable foundations.

Dickens also worked privately for certain charities, and in particular with Angela Burdett-Coutts, a wealthy philanthropist who supported a number of different charities. Dickens became her adviser and helped to administer some of her projects, most notably her 'Home for Homeless Women'.

'As a major literary figure Dickens also campaigned for certain professional causes. He spoke out strongly for a law of International Copyright, to protect authors like himself from having their works published abroad without their permission and without their earning anything from the publication. He also campaigned to raise money for impoverished actors, artists and writers.

In this chapter we will look at extracts from Dickens's journalism and speeches, and will try to build up a picture of his view of society in his lifetime.

On the fifth of last November I, the Conductor of this journal, accompanied by a friend well-known to the public, accidentally strayed into Whitechapel. It was a miserable evening; very dark, very muddy, and raining hard.

There are many woeful sights in that part of London, and it has been well-known to me in most of its aspects for many years. We had forgotten the mud and rain in slowly walking along and looking about us, when we found ourselves, at eight o'clock, before the Workhouse.

Crouched against the wall of the Workhouse, in the dark street, on the muddy pavement-stones, with the rain raining upon them, were five bundles of rags. They were motionless, and had no resemblance to the human form. Five great beehives, covered with rags – five dead bodies taken out of graves, tied neck and heels, and covered with rags – would have looked like those five bundles upon which the rain rained down in the public street.

'What is this!' said my companion. 'What *is* this!'

'Some miserable people shut out of the Casual Ward, I think,' said I.

We had stopped before the five ragged mounds, and were quite rooted to the spot by their horrible appearance. Five awful Sphinxes by the wayside,

crying to every passer-by, 'Stop and guess! What is to be the end of a state of society that leaves us here!'

As we stood looking at them, a decent working-man, having the appearance of a stone-mason, touched me on the shoulder.

'This is an awful sight, sir,' said he, 'in a Christian country!'

'God knows it is, my friend,' said I.

'I have often seen it much worse than this, as I have been going home from my work. I have counted fifteen, twenty, five-and-twenty, many a time. It's a shocking thing to see.'

'A shocking thing, indeed,' said I and my companion together. The man lingered near us a little while, wished us good-night, and went on.

We should have felt it brutal in us who had a better chance of being heard than the working-man, to leave the thing as it was, so we knocked at the Workhouse Gate. I undertook to be spokesman. The moment the gate was opened by an old pauper, I went in, followed close by my companion. I lost no time in passing the old porter, for I saw in his watery eye a disposition to shut us out.

'Be so good as to give that card to the master of the Workhouse, and say I shall be glad to speak to him for a moment.'

We were in a kind of covered gateway, and the old porter went across it with the card. Before he had got to a door on our left, a man in a cloak and hat bounced out of it very sharply, as if he were in the nightly habit of being bullied and of returning the compliment.

'Now, gentlemen,' said he in a loud voice, 'what do you want here?'

'First,' said I, 'will you do me the favour to look at that card in your hand. Perhaps you may know my name.'

'Yes,' says he, looking at it. 'I know this name.'

'Good. I only want to ask you a plain question in a civil manner, and there is not the least occasion for either of us to be angry. It would be very foolish in me to blame you, and I don't blame you. I may find fault with the system you administer, but pray understand that I know you are here to do a duty pointed out to you, and that I have no doubt you do it. Now, I hope you won't object to tell me what I want to know.'

'No,' said he, quite mollified, and very reasonable, 'not at all. What is it?'

'Do you know that there are five wretched creatures outside?'

'I haven't seen them, but I dare say there are.'

'Do you doubt that there are?'

'No, not at all. There might be many more.'

'Are they men? Or women?'

'Women, I suppose. Very likely one or two of them were there last night, and the night before last.'

'There all night, do you mean?'

'Very likely.'

My companion and I looked at one another, and the master of the Workhouse added quickly, 'Why, Lord bless my soul, what am I to do? What can I do? The place is full. The place is always full – every night. I must give the preference to women with children, mustn't I? You wouldn't have me not do that?'

'Surely not,' said I. 'It is a very humane principle, and quite right; and I am glad to hear of it. Don't forget that I don't blame *you*.'

'Well!' said he. And subdued himself again.

'What I want to ask you,' I went on, 'is whether you know anything against those five miserable beings outside?'

'Don't know anything about them,' said he, with a wave of his arm.

'I ask, for this reason: that we mean to give them a trifle to get a lodging – if they are not shelterless because they are thieves for instance. – You don't know them to be thieves?'

'I don't know anything about them,' he repeated emphatically.

'That is to say, they are shut out, solely because the Ward is full?'

'Because the Ward is full.'

'And if they get in, they would only have a roof for the night and a bit of bread in the morning, I suppose?'

'That's all. You'll use your own discretion about what you give them. Only understand that I don't know anything about them beyond what I have told you.'

'Just so. I wanted to know no more. You have answered my question civilly and readily, and I am much obliged to you. I have nothing to say against you, but quite the contrary. Good night!'

'Good night, gentlemen!' And out we came again.

We went to the ragged bundle nearest to the Workhouse-door, and I touched it. No movement replying, I gently shook it. The rags began to be slowly stirred within, and by little and little a head was unshrouded. The head of a young woman of three or four and twenty, as I should judge; gaunt with want, and foul with dirt; but not naturally ugly.

'Tell us,' said I, stooping down. 'Why are you lying here?'

'Because I can't get into the Workhouse.'

She spoke in a faint dull way, and had no curiosity or interest left. She looked dreamily at the black sky and the falling rain, but never looked at me or my companion.

'Were you here last night?'

'Yes. All last night. And the night afore too.'

'Do you know any of these others?'

'I know her next but one. She was here last night, and she told me she come out of Essex. I don't know no more of her.'

'You were here all last night, but you have not been here all day?'

'No. Not all day.'

'Where have you been all day?'

'About the streets.'

'What have you had to eat?'

'Nothing.'

'Come!' said I. 'Think a little. You are tired and have been asleep, and don't quite consider what you are saying to us. You have had something to eat to-day. Come! Think of it!'

'No I haven't. Nothing but such bits as I could pick up about the market. *Why, look at me!*'

She bared her neck, and I covered it up again.

'If you had a shilling to get some supper and a lodging, should you know where to get it!'

'Yes. I could do that.'

'For God's sake get it then!'

I put the money into her hand, and she feebly rose up and went away. She never thanked me, never looked at me — melted away into the miserable night, in the strangest manner I ever saw. I have seen many strange things, but not one that has left a deeper impression on my memory than the dull impassive way in which that worn-out heap of misery took that piece of money, and was lost.

One by one I spoke to all the five. In every one, interest and curiosity were as extinct as in the first. They were all dull and languid. No one made any sort of profession or complaint; no one cared to look at me; no one thanked me. When I came to the third, I suppose she saw that my companion and I glanced, with a new horror upon us, at the last two, who had dropped against each other in their sleep, and were lying like broken images. She said, she believed they were young sisters. These were the only words that were originated among the five.

And now let me close this terrible account with a redeeming and beautiful trait of the poorest of the poor. When we came out of the Workhouse, we had gone across the road to a public house, finding ourselves without silver, to get change for a sovereign. I held the money in my hand while I was speaking to the five apparitions. Our being so engaged, attracted the attention of many people of the very poor sort usual to that place; as we leaned over the mounds of rags, they eagerly leaned over us to see and hear; what I had in my hand, and what I said, and what I did, must have been plain to nearly all the concourse. When the last of the five had got up and faded away, the spectators opened to let us pass; and not one of them, by word, or look, or gesture, begged of us. Many of the observant faces were quick enough to know that it would have been a relief to us to have got rid of the rest of the money with any hope of doing good with it. But, there was a feeling among them all, that their necessities were not to be placed by the side of such a spectacle; and they opened a way for us in profound silence, and let us go.

From Household Words, 26 January 1856

(This piece has recently been reprinted in the anthology of Dickens's journalism *A December Vision* – see *Select bibliography* at the end of this book.)

One group of people who seemed to Dickens to be facing up to the squalor of urban life were the members of the newly constituted Detective Police. In *Reprinted Pieces* Dickens published an account of a night-time outing with a police inspector to the slums of London. After a short journey from the police station they arrive in the thick of one of London's worst slums. Dickens then asks his readers:

How many people may there be in London, who, if we had brought them deviously and blindfold, to this street, fifty paces from the Station House, and within call of Saint Giles's church, would know it for a not remote part of the city in which their lives are passed? How many, who, amidst this compound of sickening smells, these heaps of filth, these tumbling houses, with all their vile contents, animate and inanimate, slimily overflowing into the black road, would believe that they breathe *this* air? How much Red Tape may there be, that could look round on the faces which now hem us in – for our appearance here has caused a rush from all points to a common centre – the lowering foreheads, the sallow cheeks, the brutal eyes, the matted hair, the infected, vermin-haunted heaps of rags – and say 'I have thought of this. I have not dismissed the thing. I have neither blustered it away, nor frozen it away, nor tied it up and put it away, nor smoothly said pooh, pooh! to it when it has been shown to me'?

From 'On Duty with Inspector Field', in *Reprinted Pieces*

In a later piece of journalism, republished in *The Uncommercial Traveller*, we find Dickens drawing his readers' attention to similar problems of neglect and filth, but this time of children rather than streets and buildings.

Covent-garden Market, when it was market morning, was wonderful company. The great waggons of cabbages, with growers: men and boys lying asleep under them, and with sharp dogs from market-garden neighbourhoods looking after the whole, were as good as a party. But one of the worst night sights I know in London, is to be found in the children who prowl about this place; who sleep in

the baskets, fight for the offal, dart at any object they think they can lay their thieving hands on, dive under the carts and barrows, dodge the constables, and are perpetually making a blunt pattering on the pavement of the Piazza with the rain of their naked feet. A painful and unnatural result comes of the comparison one is forced to institute between the growth of corruption as displayed in the so much improved and cared for fruits of the earth, and the growth of corruption as displayed in these all uncared for (except inasmuch as ever-hunted) savages.

From 'Night Walks', in *The Uncommercial Traveller*

FOR DISCUSSION

Why do you think Dickens thought it important to present his readers with these descriptions of poverty and squalor?

WRITING

Imagine Dickens were alive today. What scenes of poverty might he focus our attention on from our society? Write a paragraph in a similar style describing a modern scene of poverty and deprivation.

Dickens had no time for the defenders of the old system, and was quick to see the necessity for proper sanitary arrangements if town-dwellers were to be protected from disease. He also recognised that the poor were always the first to suffer as their areas were always the dirtiest. In May 1851, in a speech to the Metropolitan Sanitary Association, he said:

Public health

One of the responses to the problems of poverty and disease in towns and cities was the Public Health Movement. This was led by a handful of individuals, notably Dr Thomas Southwood Smith and Edwin Chadwick, who campaigned for cleaner towns in the belief that this would greatly reduce disease and suffering, particularly among the poor. The need for clean water, proper sewers and drains, well-paved streets and the removal of rubbish may seem obvious to us today, but many people opposed this new movement. It was seen as a challenge to the old 'Vestry' system of local government, where each individual parish was responsible for its own sewers, water supply and street cleaning.

Indeed, gentlemen, I have but a few words to say, either on the needfulness of Sanitary Reform, or on the consequent usefulness of the Metropolitan Sanitary Association.

That no one can estimate the amount of mischief which is grown in dirt; that no one can say, here it stops, or there it stops, either in its physical or its moral results, when both begin in the cradle and are not at rest in the obscene grave [*hear, hear*], is now as certain as it is that the air from Gin Lane will be carried, when the wind is Easterly, into May Fair, and that if you once have a vigorous pestilence raging furiously in Saint Giles's, no mortal list of Lady Patronesses can keep it out of Almack's. [*Hear, hear.*]

Twelve or fifteen years ago, some of the first valuable reports of Mr Chadwick and of Dr South-wood Smith strengthening and much enlarging my previous imperfect knowledge of this truth, made me, in my sphere, earnest in the Sanitary Cause. And I can

Two views of the Fleet Ditch and the 'Red Lion' tavern before demolition, showing open sewers – the source of so much endemic disease in London: the back of the 'Red Lion' from the Fleet, and the Fleet Ditch from the 'Red Lion'

honestly declare tonight, that all the use I have since made of my eyes – or nose [*laughter*] – that all the information I have since been able to acquire through any of my senses, has strengthened me in the conviction that Searching Sanitary Reform must precede all other social remedies [*cheers*], and that even Education and Religion can do nothing where they are most needed, until the way is paved for their ministrations by Cleanliness and Decency. [*Hear.*] Am I singular in this opinion? You will remember the speech made this night by the Right Reverend Prelate, which no true Sanitary Reformer can have heard without emotion. [*Hear, hear.*] What avails it to send a Missionary to me, a miserable man or woman living in a fœtid Court where every sense bestowed upon me for my delight becomes a torment, and every minute of my life is new mire added to the heap under which I lie degraded? To what natural feeling within me is he to address himself? What ancient chord within me can he hope to touch? Is it my remembrance of my children? Is it a remembrance of distortion and decay, scrofula and fever? Would he address himself to my hopes of immortality? I am so surrounded by material filth that my Soul can not rise to the contemplation of an immaterial existence!

From *Collected Speeches*, 10 May 1851, pp. 28–9

He published an article in *Household Words*, republished in *Reprinted Pieces*, in which he attacked the old Vestry system of local government on a number of grounds, in particular that of public health.

. . . our Vestry shines habitually. In asserting its own pre-eminence, for instance, it is very strong. On the least provocation, or on none, it will be clamorous to know whether it is to be 'dictated to,' or 'trampled on,' or 'ridden over rough-shod.' Its great watchword is Self-government. That is to say, supposing our Vestry to favour any little harmless disorder like Typhus Fever, and supposing the Government of the country to be, by any accident, in such ridiculous hands as that any of its authorities should consider it a duty to object to Typhus Fever – obviously an unconstitutional objection – then, our Vestry cuts in with a terrible manifesto about Self-government, and claims its independent right to have as much Typhus Fever as pleases itself. Some absurd and dangerous persons have represented on the other hand, that though our Vestry may be able to 'beat the bounds' of its own parish, it may not be able to beat the bounds of its own diseases; which (say they) spread over the whole land, in an ever-expanding circle of waste, and misery, and death, and widowhood, and orphanage, and desolation. But, our Vestry makes short work of any such fellows as these.

It was our Vestry – pink of Vestries as it is – that in support of its favourite principle took the celebrated ground of denying the existence of the last pestilence that raged in England, when the pestilence was raging at the Vestry doors. Dogginson said it was plums; Mr Wigsby (of Chumbledon Square) said it was oysters; Mr Magg (of Little Winkling Street) said, amid great cheering, it was the newspapers.

From 'Our Vestry', in *Reprinted Pieces*

FOR DISCUSSION

1 What reasons does Dickens give here for supporting the Public Health Movement?
2 What criticisms does Dickens make of the Vestry system?

There were other problems faced by town-dwellers. Slaughter-houses were often found in the middle of densely populated areas, as were many overflowing graveyards. Both of these presented acute health hazards and Dickens campaigned against them. Part of the story of *Bleak House* concerns the spread of disease from a graveyard in the heart of London. Dickens dedicated a whole article in *Household Words* to contrasting the bad English system of slaughter-houses with the well-organised French system. He called the article, ironically, 'A Monument of French Folly' and presented his argument in terms of mock support for the 'good old English' system.

Possibly the merits of our slaughter-houses are not yet quite so generally appreciated. Slaughter-houses, in the large towns of England, are always (with the exception of one or two enterprising towns) most numerous in the most densely crowded places, where there is the least circulation of air. They are often underground, in cellars; they are sometimes in close back-yards; sometimes (as in Spitalfields) in the very shops where the meat is sold. Occasionally, under good private management, they are ventilated and clean. For the most part, they are unventilated and dirty; and, to the reeking walls, putrid fat and other offensive animal matter clings with a tenacious hold. The busiest slaughter-houses in London are in the neighbourhood of Smithfield, in Newgate Market, in Whitechapel, in Newport Market, in Leadenhall Market, in Clare Market. All these places are surrounded by houses of a poor description, swarming with inhabitants. Some of them are close to the worst burial-grounds in London. When the slaughter-house is below the ground, it is a common practice to throw the sheep down areas, neck and crop – which is exciting, but not at all cruel. When it is on the level surface, it is often extremely difficult of approach. Then, the beasts have to be worried, and goaded, and pronged, and tail-twisted, for a long time before they can be got in – which is entirely owing to their natural obstinacy. When it is not difficult of approach, but is in a foul condition, what they see and scent makes them still more reluctant to enter – which is their natural obstinacy again. When they do get in at last, after no trouble and suffering to speak of (for, there is nothing in the previous journey into the heart of London, the night's endurance in Smithfield, the struggle out again, among the crowded multitude, the coaches, carts, waggons, omnibuses, gigs, chaises, phaetons, cabs, trucks, dogs, boys, whoopings, roarings, and ten thousand other distractions), they are represented to be in a most unfit state to be killed, according to microscopic examinations made of their fevered blood by one of the most distinguished physiologists in the world, Professor Owen – but that's humbug. When they *are* killed, at last, their reeking carcases are hung in impure air, to become, as the same Professor will explain to you, less nutritious and more unwholesome – but he is only an *un*common counsellor, so don't mind *him*. In half a quarter of a mile's length of Whitechapel, at one time, there shall be six hundred newly slaughtered oxen hanging up, and seven hundred sheep – but, the more the merrier – proof of prosperity. Hard by Snow Hill and Warwick Lane, you shall see the little children, inured to sights of brutality from their birth, trotting along the alleys, mingled with troops of horribly busy pigs, up to their ankles in blood – but it makes the young rascals hardy. Into the imperfect sewers of this overgrown city, you shall have the immense mass of corruption, engendered by these practices, lazily thrown out of sight, to rise in poisonous gases, into your house at night, when your sleeping children will most readily absorb them, and to find its languid way, at last, into the river that you drink – but, the French are a frog-eating people who wear wooden shoes, and it's O the roast beef of England, my boy, the jolly old English roast beef.

It is quite a mistake – a new fangled notion altogether – to suppose that there is any natural antagonism between putrefaction and health. They know better than that, in the Common Council. You may talk about Nature, in her wisdom, always warning man through his sense of smell, when he draws near to something dangerous; but, that won't go down in the City. Nature very often don't mean anything. Mrs Quickly says that prunes are ill for a green wound; but whosoever says that putrid animal substances are ill for a green wound, or for robust vigour, or for anything or for anybody, is a humanity-monger and a humbug. Britons never, never, never, etc., therefore. And prosperity to cattle-driving, cattle-slaughtering, bone-crushing, blood-boiling, trotter-scraping, tripe-dressing, paunch-cleaning, gut-spinning, hide-preparing, tallow-melting, and other salubrious proceedings, in the midst of hospitals, churchyards, workhouses, schools, infirmaries, refuges, dwellings, provision-shops, nurseries, sick-beds, every stage and baiting-place in the journey from birth to death!

From 'A Monument to French Folly', *Reprinted Pieces*

Dickens, like many of his contemporaries, thought that diseases such as typhoid and cholera were transmitted through 'foul air' – that is, disease was carried with smells. By the mid-1850s, Dr John Snow was arguing that these diseases were in fact carried in water. Even after Snow had proved his point, many people continued to believe in the need for 'pure' air and the dangerous effects of smells. Both groups agreed, and were right, over the need for greater public cleanliness.

Cholera was a deadly disease that swept through Europe in the early 1830s, late 1840s and mid-1850s. It spread rapidly and mysteriously – we now know it was spread through contaminated water – and killed thousands of people. It arrived in this country in 1831 and again at the end of 1848. Measures were taken to combat it, but these were often ineffectual. As always the disease raged most fiercely amongst the poor: their streets and houses were filthier and their bodies less resistant to disease than those of their wealthier fellow-citizens.

When cholera broke out at Mr Drouet's Home for Pauper Children, the parish churchyard soon became too small for the piles of children's coffins. Drouet's 'Baby Farm' was a place where local authorities sent the very young children who came into their care. (You may remember that Oliver

Twist spent his first nine years at Mrs Mann's 'Baby Farm'.) Fourteen hundred children lived on Drouet's 'Farm' and the terrible conditions under which they lived made them very vulnerable to the disease when it broke out.

Dickens was furious, particularly at the casual attitude of the Poor Law Guardians (officials) and the Surrey Coroner, who were all quite prepared to believe that all was as it should be at Drouet's establishment. Dickens was pleased to be able to support the new Board of Health in its criticisms of the Metropolitan Board of Guardians. He wrote a series of articles for *The Examiner* while the case was being fought out in the Coroner's Court. The first article was entitled 'The Paradise at Tooting' and Dickens starts off in a strongly ironic tone.

THE PARADISE AT TOOTING

When it first became known that a virulent and fatal epidemic had broken out in Mr Drouet's farming establishment for pauper children at Tooting, the comfortable flourish of trumpets usual on such occasions (Sydney Smith's admirable description of it will be fresh in the minds of many of our readers) was performed as a matter of course. Of all similar establishments on earth, that at Tooting was the most admirable. Of all similar contractors on earth, Mr Drouet was the most disinterested, zealous, and unimpeachable. Of all the wonders ever wondered at, nothing perhaps had ever occurred more wonderful than the outbreak and rapid increase of a disorder so horrible, in a place so perfectly regulated. There was no warning of its approach. Nothing was less to be expected. The farmed children were slumbering in the lap of peace and plenty; Mr Drouet, the farmer, was slumbering with an easy conscience, but with one eye perpetually open, to keep watch upon the blessings he diffused, and upon the happy infants under his paternal charge; when, in a moment the destroyer was upon them, and Tooting churchyard became too small for the piles of children's coffins that were carried out of this Elysium every day.

The learned coroner for the county of Surrey deemed it quite unnecessary to hold any inquests on these dead children, being as perfectly satisfied in his own mind that Mr Drouet's farm was the best of all possible farms.

However, the Surrey Coroner did not have the last word, as some of the children who had died were the concern of another county's coroner. Dickens continues his article:

. . . we will refer to the proceedings before a very different kind of coroner, Mr Wakley, and his deputy Mr Mills. But that certain of the miserable little creatures removed from Tooting happened to die within Mr Wakley's jurisdiction, it is by no means unlikely that a committee might have sprung into existence by this time, for presenting Mr Drouet with some magnificent testimonial, as a mark of public respect and sympathy.

Mr Wakley, however, being of little faith, holds inquests, and even manifests a disposition to institute a very searching inquiry into the causes of these horrors; rather thinking that such grievous effects must have some grievous causes. Remembering that there is a public institution called the 'Board of Health', Mr Wakley summons before him Dr Grainger, an inspector acting under that board, who has examined Mr Drouet's Elysium, and has drawn up a report concerning it.

It then comes out – truth is so perverse – that Mr Drouet is not altogether that golden farmer he was supposed to be. It appears that there is a little alloy in his composition. The 'extreme closeness, oppression, and foulness of air' in that supposed heaven upon earth over which he presides, 'exceeds in offensiveness anything ever yet witnessed by the inspector, in apartments in hospitals, or elsewhere, occupied by the sick.' He had a bad habit of putting four cholera patients in one bed. He has a weakness in respect of leaving the sick to take care of themselves, surrounded by every offensive, indecent, and barbarous circumstance that can aggravate the horrors of their condition and increase the dangers of infection. He is so ignorant, or so criminally careless, that he has taken none of the easy precautions, and provided himself with none of the simple remedies expressly enjoined by the Board of Health in their official announcement published in the *Gazette*, and distributed all over the country. The experience of all the medical observers of cholera, in all parts of the world, is not in an instant overthrown by Mr Drouet's purity, for he had unfortunately one fortnight's warning of the impending danger, which he utterly disregarded. He has been admonished by the authorities to take only a certain number of unfortunates into his farm, and he increases that number immensely at his own pleasure, for his own profit. His establishment is crammed. It is in no respect a fit place for the reception of the throng shut up in it. The dietary of the children is so unwholesome and insufficient, that they climb secretly over palings, and pick out scraps of sustenance from the tubs of hog-wash. Their clothing by day, and their covering by night, are shamefully defective. Their rooms are cold, damp, dirty, and rotten. In a word, the age of miracles is past, and of all conceivable places in which pestilence might – or rather *must* – be expected to break out, and to make direful ravages, Mr Drouet's model farm stands foremost.

Dickens goes on to explain how Drouet managed to keep all this quiet: by intimidating staff and children, and through the laziness of the Poor Law Guardians, some of whom encouraged Drouet in his harsh treatment of the children.

Dickens concludes his article with a forceful summing up. First he summarises the position of the Board of Guardians:

E verything was comfortable and pleasant. Of all places in the world, how could the cholera ever break out, after this, in Mr Drouet's Paradise at Tooting!

He then gives the Board of Health's position, which he presents as a reply to the above question:

B ut the Board of Health – an institution of which every day's experience attests in some new form the value and importance – has settled the question. Plainly thus: – The cholera, or some unusually malignant form of typhus assimilating itself to that disease, broke out in Mr Drouet's farm for children, because it was brutally conducted, vilely kept, preposterously inspected, dishonestly defended, a disgrace to a Christian community, and a stain upon a civilised land.

From *The Examiner*, 20 January 1849

A week later, following the verdict of the coroner's court, that Drouet was guilty of manslaughter, Dickens published a short article in the *Examiner* in which he voiced the following opinion:

I f the system of farming pauper children cannot exist without the danger of another Tooting Farm being weeded by the grisly hands of Want, Disease and Death, let it now be abolished.

From *The Examiner*, 27 January 1849

WRITING

Imagine a campaign is launched to scrap the system of 'farming' pauper children, following the Drouet case. Write a leaflet encouraging members of the public to join the campaign. Give examples, from the Drouet case, of the evils of the system.

FURTHER READING

Chapters 11 and 16 of *Bleak House*, describing a city graveyard.

Education

Throughout his career Dickens campaigned fiercely against bad schools and strongly supported those schools and institutions which he considered valuable. In 1843, quite early in his career as a speechmaker and commentator, we find him defending the cause of popular education in a speech to the Manchester Athenaeum. This was an institution for adult education which Dickens continued to support over the ensuing years.

One of the arguments that Dickens used on this occasion was that ignorance was the parent of crime. He was struck by the fact that the state entered into poor people's lives only in order to punish them. He also believed that a great deal of crime could be avoided if the state bothered to educate *all* its citizens. (We should remember that free education for all only started in 1870 – the year of Dickens's death.)

In February 1846, Dickens wrote a piece for the *Daily News* in which he drew his readers' attention to the Ragged Schools, which were free schools set up by religious people in the poorest areas of London. He opens with the following paragraphs:

CRIME AND EDUCATION

I offer no apology for entreating the attention of the readers of the *Daily News* to an effort which has been making for some three years and a half, and which is making now, to introduce among the most miserable and neglected outcasts in London some knowledge of the commonest principles of morality and religion; to commence their recognition as immortal human creatures, before the jail Chaplain becomes their only schoolmaster; to suggest to Society that its duty to this wretched throng, foredoomed to crime and punishment, rightfully begins at some distance from the police office; and that the careless maintenance from year to year, in this the capital city of the world, of a vast, hopeless nursery of ignorance, misery, and vice – a breeding place for the hulks and jails – is horrible to contemplate.

This attempt is being made, in certain of the most obscure and squalid parts of the Metropolis; where rooms are opened, at night, for the gratuitous instruction of all comers, children or adults, under the title of *Ragged Schools*. The name implies the purpose. They

Ragged schools were set up in some of the poorest areas of London in the mid-nineteenth century

who are too ragged, wretched, filthy, and forlorn, to enter any other place; who could gain admission into no charity school, and who would be driven from any church-door, are invited to come in here, and find some people not depraved, willing to teach them something, and show them some sympathy, and stretch out a hand, which is not the iron hand of Law, for their correction.

He goes on to argue that crime and ignorance are firmly linked, not only in his opinion but also in the opinion of two prison governors. He then describes his visit to the Field Lane Ragged School.

It consisted at that time of either two or three – I forget which – miserable rooms, upstairs in a miserable house. In the best of these, the pupils in the female school were being taught to read and write; and, though there were among the number many wretched creatures steeped in degradation to the lips, they were tolerably quiet, and listened with apparent earnestness and patience to their instructors. The appearance of this room was sad and melancholy, of course – how could it be otherwise! – but, on the whole, encouraging.

The close, low chamber at the back, in which the boys were crowded, was so foul and stifling as to be, at first, almost insupportable. But its moral aspect was so far worse than its physical that this was soon forgotten. Huddled together on a bench about the room, and shown out by some flaring candles stuck against the walls, were a crowd of boys, varying from mere infants to young men; sellers of fruit, herbs, lucifer-matches, flints; sleepers under the dry arches of bridges; young thieves and beggars – with nothing natural to youth about them: with nothing frank, ingenuous, or pleasant in their faces; low-browed, vicious, cunning, wicked; abandoned of all help but this; speeding down-wards to destruction; and *Unutterably Ignorant*.

. . . This was the Class I saw at the Ragged School. They could not be trusted with books; they could only be instructed orally; they were difficult of reduction to anything like attention, obedience, or decent behaviour; their benighted ignorance in reference to the Deity, or to any social duty (how could they guess at any social duty, being so discarded by all social teachers but the jailer and the hangman!) was terrible to see. Yet, even here, and among these, something had been done already. The Ragged School was of recent date and very poor; but it had inculcated some association with the name of the Almighty which was not an oath, and had taught them to look forward in a hymn (they sang it) to another life which would correct the miseries and woes of this.

The new exposition I found in this Ragged School of the frightful neglect by the State of those whom it punishes so constantly, and whom it might, as easily and less expensively, instruct and save, together with the sight I had seen there, in the heart of London, haunted me, and finally impelled me to an endeavour to bring these Institutions under the notice of the Government; with some faint hope that the vastness of the question would supersede the theology of the schools, and that the Bench of Bishops might adjust the latter question, after some small grant had been conceded. I made the attempt; and have heard no more of the subject, from that hour.

From *Daily News*, 4 February 1846

Note: Dickens's reference to the problem of the 'theology of the schools' points very clearly to the problem such schools faced. The Church of England was the chief source of funds for the education of the poor, and religious disputes often meant that particular schools preaching particular doctrines would not receive funds. It was disputes such as these, principally between the Church of England and the non-conformist churches, which proved the biggest stumbling block to the setting up of free education. The wrangling started in the mid-1840s and went on until 1870.

FOR DISCUSSION

1 What do you think Dickens found 'encouraging' about the school?
2 Why do you think the young people went to the school? (Remember, they all had some sort of job and the school met in the evening. It was also voluntary.)

DRAMA SUGGESTION

Imagine what the young people felt and said when their visitors arrived. What did the teacher do? How did Dickens behave? Try re-enacting this meeting between the famous novelist and the Ragged School class.

Dickens continued to support and advise the Ragged Schools, and also persuaded Miss Burdett-Coutts (a wealthy philanthropist) to give them some financial support. With her help the Field Lane School hired new premises which, on Dickens's insistence, contained washing facilities for the pupils.

Dickens supported many other educational institutions through his speeches and journalism. These included the Liverpool Mechanics Institution, the Polytechnic Institution of Birmingham, the Manchester Free Library and the Leeds Mechanics Institution. (You can read for yourself what he had to say to many of these in the *Collected Speeches* – see *Select bibliography* at the end of this book.)

Dickens kept a critical eye on education. One development he particularly disliked was that of factory schools, about which he wrote at length in his novel *Hard Times* (see Chapters 1 and 2). In a speech made shortly after writing *Hard Times*, he summarised his criticisms of a number of types of school and included these comments on the factory schools.

I don't like that sort of school – and I have seen a great many such in these latter times – where the bright childish imagination is utterly discouraged, and where those bright childish faces, which it is so very good for the wisest among us to remember in after life [*hear, hear*], when the world is too much with us early and late, are gloomily and grimly scared out of countenance; where I have never seen among the pupils, whether boys or girls, anything but little parrots and small calculating machines.

From *Collected Speeches*, 5 November 1857, p. 241

<hr>

FOR DISCUSSION

Why does Dickens describe the pupils as 'little parrots and small calculating machines'? What does this tell us about the sort of education they were receiving?

<hr>

In a speech made during the last few months of his life, to the Birmingham and Midland Institute, Dickens offered the following thought about study and the process of learning.

The one serviceable, safe, certain, remunerative, attainable quality in every study and in every pursuit is the quality of attention. My own invention or imagination, such as it is, I can most truthfully assure you, would never have served me as it has, but for the habit of commonplace, humble, patient, daily, toiling, drudging attention. [*Applause.*] Genius, vivacity, quickness of penetration, brilliancy in association of ideas – such mental qualities, like the qualities of the apparition of the externally armed head in *Macbeth* will not be commanded; but attention, after due term of submissive service, always will. Like certain plants which the poorest peasant may grow in the poorest soil, it can be cultivated by anyone, and it is certain in its own good season to bring forth flowers and fruit.

From *Collected Speeches*, 27 September 1869, p. 406

(There was no false modesty here: Dickens was a writer of genius and energy, but he was also very regular in his working habits and wrote his novels at a steady pace – the usual pattern was three pages a day for two weeks every month.)

<hr>

FOR DISCUSSION

1 Why is this point about 'attention', or application as we might say nowadays, an important argument in the campaign for education for all?
2 Why does Dickens compare 'attention' to a plant 'raised by the poorest peasant in the poorest soil'?

<hr>

We have looked at some of Dickens's pronouncements on education. He was clearly interested in a wide range of educational developments, criticising and supporting energetically a large number of different institutions and systems of education.

<hr>

WRITING

What sort of comments might Dickens have made after a visit to *your* school? Write an article, as if you were Dickens, in which you discuss the good and bad aspects of your present school. Try to achieve something of his forceful, penetrating style!

Crime

Dickens had a keen interest in questions of crime and the treatment of criminals. He wrote about criminals with insight and conviction in *Oliver Twist*, where he created Bill Sikes and Fagin – two of English literature's most notorious characters.

He was also interested in prisons and systems designed to reform young criminals and punish hardened ones. When in America he made visits to a number of penitentiaries and reformatories. He was friendly with two prison governors in London, Lieutenant Tracey and G. L. Chesterton. He also met and was influenced by Captain Macconochie, the pioneering governor of the British Penal Colony, Norfolk Island, in the Pacific Ocean.

In March 1846, Dickens wrote a series of three letters to the *Daily News*. His letters were all on the question of capital punishment. In those days, we should remember, hangings were public occasions which drew large crowds. Dickens was very critical of this.

We come, now, to consider the effect of Capital Punishment in the prevention of crime.

Does it prevent crime in those who attend executions?

There never is (and there never was) an execution at the Old Bailey in London, but the spectators include two large classes of thieves – one class who go there as they would go to a dog-fight, or any other brutal sport, for the attraction and excitement of the spectacle; the other who make it a dry matter of business, and mix with the crowd solely to pick pockets. Add to these, the dissolute, the drunken, the most idle, profligate, and abandoned of both sexes – some moody, ill-conditioned minds, drawn thither by a fearful interest – and some impelled by curiosity; of whom the greatest part are of an age and temperament rendering the gratification of that curiosity highly dangerous to themselves and to society – and the great elements of the concourse are stated.

Nor is this assemblage peculiar to London. It is the same in country towns, allowing for the different

Newgate Prison in London

statistics of the population. It is the same in America. I was present at an execution in Rome, for a most treacherous and wicked murder, and . . . saw the same kind of assemblage there . . . .

I have already mentioned that out of one hundred and sixty-seven convicts under sentence of death, questioned at different times in the performance of his duty by an English clergyman, there were only three who had not been spectators of executions.

From *Daily News*, 13 March 1846

FOR DISCUSSION

1 What do you think Dickens means by 'the most idle, profligate, and abandoned of both sexes'?
2 What overall impression does he create of a public hanging?
3 What is significant about the statistic of convicts under sentence of death and attendance at public executions?

Dickens became involved in the debate over how prisoners should be treated. There were two schools of thought at the time: one allowed prisoners to mix with each other but insisted on silence; the other believed in keeping prisoners in solitary confinement so that they could think about their crimes and reform their characters. Dickens found this latter system at work in America and he vigorously opposed it as he saw that the constant isolation reduced prisoners to mental wrecks. He remained dubious about the idea of criminals 'reforming' in prison and believed that such a system encouraged fake reformations. He wrote this into *David Copperfield*, Chapter 61, when Uriah Heep reappears as a 'penitent' prisoner.

As Dickens grew older his attitude towards criminals became more severe. One of his later articles, written for his magazine *All The Year Round* and republished in *The Uncommercial Traveller*, starts with the following 'hard-line' approach to the problem of what our press would now call 'muggers'.

THE RUFFIAN

I entertain so strong an objection to the euphonious softening of Ruffian into Rough, which has lately become popular, that I restore the right word to the heading of this paper; the rather, as my object is to dwell upon the fact that the Ruffian is tolerated among us to an extent that goes beyond all unruffianly endurance. I take the liberty to believe that if the Ruffian besets my life, a professional Ruffian at large in the open streets of a great city, notoriously having no other calling than that of Ruffian, and of disquieting and despoiling me as I go peacefully about my lawful business, interfering with no one, then the Government under which I have the great constitutional privilege, supreme honour and happiness, and all the rest of it, to exist, breaks down in the discharge of any Government's most simple elementary duty.

What did I read in the London daily papers, in the early days of last September? That the Police had 'AT LENGTH SUCCEEDED IN CAPTURING TWO OF THE NOTORIOUS GANG THAT HAVE SO LONG INFESTED THE WATERLOO ROAD.' Is it possible? What a wonderful Police! Here is a straight, broad, public thoroughfare of immense resort; half a mile long; gas-lighted by night; with a great gas-lighted railway station in it, extra the street-lamps; full of shops; traversed by two popular cross thoroughfares of considerable traffic; itself the main road to the south of London; and the admirable Police have, after long infestment of this dark and lonely spot by a gang of Ruffians, actually got hold of two of them. Why, can it be doubted that any man of fair London knowledge and common resolution, armed with the powers of the Law, could have captured the whole confederacy in a week?

It is to the saving up of the Ruffian class by the Magistracy and Police – to the conventional preserving of them, as if they were Partridges – that their number and audacity must be in great part referred. Why is a notorious Thief and Ruffian ever left at large? He never turns his liberty to any account by violence and plunder, he never did a day's work out of gaol, he never will do a day's work out of gaol. As a proved notorious Thief he is always consignable to prison for three months. When he comes out, he is surely as notorious a Thief as he was when he went in. Then send him back again. 'Just Heaven!' cries the Society for the protection of remonstrant Ruffians. 'This is equivalent to a sentence of perpetual imprisonment!' Precisely for that reason it has my advocacy. I demand to have the Ruffian kept out of my way, and out of the way of all decent people. I demand to have the Ruffian employed, perforce, in hewing wood and drawing water somewhere for the general service, instead of hewing at her Majesty's subjects and drawing their watches out of their pockets. If this be termed an unreasonable demand, then the tax-gatherer's demand on me must be far more unreasonable, and cannot be otherwise than extortionate and unjust.

It will be seen that I treat of the Thief and Ruffian as one. I do so, because I know the two characters to be one, in the vast majority of cases, just as well as the Police know it. (As to the Magistracy, with a few exceptions, they know nothing about it but what the Police choose to tell them.) There are disorderly classes of men who are not thieves; as railway-navigators, brickmakers, wood-sawyers, coster-mongers. These classes are often disorderly and troublesome; but it is mostly among themselves, and at any rate they have their industrious avocations, they work early and late, and work hard. The generic Ruffian – honourable member for what is tenderly called the Rough Element – is either a Thief, or the companion of Thieves. When he infamously molests women coming out of chapel on Sunday evenings (for which I would have his back scarified often and deep) it is not only for the gratification of his pleasant instincts, but that there may be a confusion raised by which either he or his friends may profit, in the commission of highway robberies or in picking pockets. When he gets a police constable down and kicks him helpless for life, it is because that constable once did his duty in bringing him to justice. When he rushes into the bar of a public-house and scoops an eye out of one of the company there, or bites his ear off, it is because the man he maims gave evidence against him. When he and a line of comrades extending across the footway – say of that solitary mountain-spur of the Abruzzi, the Waterloo Road – advance towards me 'skylarking' among themselves, my purse or shirt-pin is in predestined peril from his playfulness. Always a Ruffian always a Thief. Always a Thief, always a Ruffian.

From *The Uncommercial Traveller*, Ch. 30

FOR DISCUSSION

1 On what grounds does Dickens argue for the arrest and imprisonment of known 'ruffians'?
2 What criticisms might one make of these ideas?

Missionaries

One of the concerns of the Church in the mid-nineteenth century was with missionary work, particularly in Africa, India and the Far East.

Dickens's attitude to missionary work is very clear in the following extract from a long article written in August 1848 for *The Examiner*. In it he discusses the history of a recent Government expedition to Africa. The expedition was designed to help put down the slave trade in Africa and, at the same time, to establish Christianity and trading relations in Obi's kingdom in West Africa. The expedition was a disaster. Many of the men died from fever, promises were not kept and nothing was achieved.

After writing a summary of events, Dickens commented:

The history of this Expedition is the history of the Past, in reference to the heated visions of philanthropists for the railroad Christianisation of Africa and the abolition of the Slave-trade. May no popular cry, from Exeter Hall or elsewhere, ever make it, as to one single ship, the history of the future! Such means are useless, futile, and we will venture to add – in despite of hats broad-brimmed or shovel-shaped, and coats of drab or black, with collars or without – indeed. No amount of philanthropy has a right to waste such valuable life as was squandered here, in the teeth of all experience and feasible pretence of hope. Between the civilised European and the barbarous African there is a great gulf set.

The air that brings life to the latter brings death to the former. In the mighty revolutions of the wheel of time, some change in this regard may come about; but in this age of the world, all the white armies and white missionaries of the world would fall, as withered reeds, before the rolling of one African river. To change the customs even of civilised and educated men, and impress them with new ideas, is – we have good need to know it – a most difficult and slow proceeding; but to do this by ignorant and savage races is a work which, like the progressive changes of the globe itself, requires a stretch of years that dazzles in the looking at. It is not, we conceive, within the likely providence of God that Christianity shall start to the banks of the Niger, until it shall have overflowed all intervening space. The stone that is dropped into the ocean of ignorance at Exeter Hall must make its widening circles, one beyond another, until they reach the negroes' country in their natural expansion. There is a broad, dark sea between the Strand in London, and the Niger, where those rings are not yet shining; and through all that space they must appear, before the last one breaks upon the shore of Africa. Gently and imperceptibly the widening circle of enlightenment must stretch and stretch, from man to man, from people on to people, until there is a girdle round the earth; but no convulsive effort, no far-off aim, can make the last great outside one first, and then come home at leisure to trace out the inner one. Believe it, African civilisation, Church of England Missionary, and all other missionary societies! The work at home must be completed thoroughly or there is no hope abroad. To your tents, O Israel! but see they are your own tents! Set *them* in order; leave nothing to be done *there*; and outpost will convey your lesson on to outpost until the naked armies of King Obi and King Boy are reached and taught. Let a knowledge of the duty that man owes to man, and to his God, spread thus, by natural degrees and growth of example, to the outer shores of Africa, and it will float in safety up the rivers, never fear!

From 'A Narrative of the Niger Expedition', *The Examiner*,
19 August 1848

FOR DISCUSSION

1 What attitudes towards the Africans does Dickens have *in common* with the missionaries?
2 What do you think Dickens means by 'the railroad Christianisation of Africa'? Why 'railroad'?
3 What criticisms might we, as modern readers, make of the ideas in this article about 'civilisation'?

FURTHER READING

Dickens continued to criticise those who were more concerned with overseas missionary work than with problems closer to home. See *Bleak House*, Chapter 4, for further comments on 'telescopic philanthropy'.

Temperance

One of the ideas Dickens consistently campaigned against was the 'temperance' movement. This movement tried to combat alcoholism by preaching the gospel of 'total abstinence' – that is to say, persuading people not to drink any alcohol whatsoever. Young people were encouraged to sign the pledge, never to take up drinking.

Alcoholism certainly was a problem in the nineteenth century. Living conditions for the poor were very bad, and cheap gin provided an easy escape for many desperate people.

Dickens was convinced that moderate drinking was an innocent pleasure and he argued against the temperance movement on many occasions. The following extracts are from an article he wrote for *Household Words*.

WHOLE HOGS

The public market has been of late more than usually remarkable for transactions on the American principle in Whole and indivisible Hogs. The market has been heavy – not the least approach to briskness having been observed in any part of it; but the transactions, such as they have been, have been exclusively for Whole Hogs. Those who may only have had a retail inclination for sides, ribs, limbs, cheeks, face, trotters, snout, ears, or tail, have been required to take the Whole Hog, sinking none of the offal, but consenting to it all – and a good deal of it too.

It has been discovered that mankind at large can only be regenerated by a Teatotal Society, or by a Peace Society, or by always dining on Vegetables. It is to be particularly remarked that either of these certain means of regeneration is utterly defeated, if so much as a hair's breadth of the tip of either ear of that particular Pig be left out of the bargain. Qualify your water with a teaspoonful of wine or brandy – we beg your pardon, alcohol – and there is no virtue in Temperance. Maintain a single sentry at the gate of the Queen's Palace, and it is utterly impossible that you can be peaceful. Stew so much as the bone of a mutton chop in the pot with your vegetables, and you will never make another Eden out of a Kitchen Garden. You must take the whole Hog, Sir, and every bristle on him, or you and the rest of mankind will never be regenerated.

* * *

... In the speeches of the ... Regenerators, Society is denounced as being wrongfully and wickedly combined against their own particular Whole Hog – who must be swallowed, every bristle, or there is no Pork in him.

The proof? Society won't come in and sign the pledge; Society won't come in and recruit the Juvenile Temperance Bands of Hope. Therefore Society is fond of drunkenness, sees no harm in it, favours it very much, *is* a drunkard – a base, worthless, sensual, profligate brute. Fathers and mothers, sons and daughters, brothers and sisters, divines, physicians, lawyers, editors, authors, painters, poets, musicians, Queens, lords, ladies, and commons, are all in the league against the Regenerators, are all violently attached to drunkenness, are all the more dangerous if by any chance they be personal examples of temperance, in the real meaning of the word! – which last powerful steam-hammer of logic has become a pet one, and is constantly to be observed in action.

Against this sweeping misrepresentation, I take the liberty of entering my feeble protest.

From *Household Words*, 23 August 1851

Dickens continued to protest. In the final chapter of *The Uncommercial Traveller* you can find another attack on the temperance movement. This later piece, 'A Plea for Total Abstinence' was written nearly nineteen years later. On this issue, at least, Dickens remained consistent!

Administrative reform

Dickens was a frequent critic, in his novels and in his journalism, of maladministration by central or local government officials. In satirising the inefficiency and self-importance of officials he invented a phrase which was quickly taken up by other writers and has since entered our language.

RED TAPE

Your public functionary who delights in Red Tape – the purpose of whose existence is to tie up public questions, great and small, in an abundance of this official article – to make the neatest possible parcels of them, ticket them, and carefully put them away on a top shelf out of human reach – is the peculiar curse and nuisance of England. Iron, steel, adamant, can make no such drag-chain as Red Tape. An invasion of Red Ants in innumerable millions, would not be half so prejudicial to Great Britain, as its intolerable Red Tape.

Your Red Tapist is everywhere. He is always at hand, with a coil of Red Tape, prepared to make a small official parcel of the largest subject. In the reception-room of a Government Office, he will wind Red Tape round and round the sternest deputation that the country can send to him. In either House of Parliament, he will pull more Red Tape out of his mouth, at a moment's notice, than a conjuror at a Fair. In letters, memoranda, and dispatches, he will spin himself into Red Tape, by the thousand yards. He will bind you up vast colonies, in Red Tape, like cold roast chickens at a rout-supper; and when the most valuable of them break it (a mere question of time), he will be amazed to find that they were too expansive for his favourite commodity. He will put a girdle of Red Tape round the earth, in quicker time than Ariel. He will measure, from Downing Street to the North Pole, or the heart of New Zealand, or the highest summit of the Himalaya Mountains, by inches of Red Tape. He will rig all the ships in the British Navy with it, weave all the colours in the British Army from it, completely equip and fit out the officers and men of both services in it. He bound Nelson and Wellington hand and foot with it – ornamented them, all over, with bunches of it – and sent them forth to do impossibilities. He will stand over the side of the steamship of the state, sounding with Red Tape, for imaginary obstacles; and when the office-seal at the end of his pet line touches a floating weed, will cry majestically, 'Back her! Stop her!' He hangs great social efforts, in Red Tape, about the public offices, to terrify like evil-minded reformers, as great highwaymen used to be hanged in chains on Hounslow Heath. He has but one answer to every demonstration of right, or exposition of wrong; and it is, 'My good Sir, this is a question of Tape.'

He is the most gentlemanly of men. He is mysterious; but not more so than a man who is cognisant of so much Tape ought to be. Butterflies and gadflies who disport themselves, unconscious of the amount of Red Tape required to keep Creation together, may wear their hearts upon their sleeves; but he is another sort of person. Not that he is wanting in conversation. By no means. Every question mooted, he has to tie up according to form, and put away. Church, state, territory native and foreign, ignorance, poverty, crime, punishment, popes, cardinals, jesuits, taxes, agriculture and commerce, land and sea – all Tape. 'Nothing but Tape, Sir, I assure you. Will you allow me to tie this subject up, with a few years, according to the official form? Thank you. Thus, you see. A knot here; the end cut off there; a twist in this place; a loop in that. Nothing can be more complete. Quite compact, you observe. I ticket it, you perceive, and put it on the shelf. It is now disposed of. What is the next article?'

The quantity of Red Tape officially employed in the defence of such an imposition (in more senses than one) as the Window Tax; the array of Red Tapists and the amount of Red Taping employed in its behalf, within the last six or seven years, is something so astounding in itself, and so illustrative of the enormous quantities of Tape devoted to the public confusion, that we take the liberty, at this appropriate time, of disentangling an odd thousand fathoms or so, as a sample of the commodity.

From *Household Words*, 15 February 1851

Note: Red tape is a type of ribbon used by officials and lawyers to bind papers together.

The article goes on to describe the inefficiency and bungling accompanying an attempt to change the Window Tax.

Like many other people Dickens was outraged at the shambolic conduct of the Crimean War (1854–56). Unlike previous wars this one was carefully reported in *The Times* and many civilians were shocked by the reports of chaos and mismanagement. A pressure group was set up to campaign for better administration in Government – The Administrative Reform Association – and Dickens assisted them in their efforts to improve Government efficiency.

During the years 1855–7 Dickens was writing and publishing his novel *Little Dorrit*. This novel includes many criticisms of the Government and Civil Service. It is interesting to note that the title he almost gave the novel was *Nobody's Fault*, and while he was working on the novel he wrote the following cover article for *Household Words*,, in which he focused on the issue of responsibility in public life.

NOBODY, SOMEBODY, AND EVERYBODY

The power of Nobody is becoming so enormous in England, and he alone is responsible for so many proceedings, both in the way of commission and omission; he has so much to answer for, and is so constantly called to account; that a few remarks upon him may not be ill-timed.

The hand which this surprising person had in the late war is amazing to consider. It was he who left the tents behind, who left the baggage behind, who chose the worst possible ground for encampments, who provided no means of transport, who killed the horses, who paralysed the commissariat, who knew nothing of the business he professed to know and monopolised, who decimated the English army. It was Nobody who gave out the famous unroasted coffee, it was Nobody who made the hospitals more horrible than language can describe, it was Nobody who occasioned all the dire confusion of Balaklava harbour, it was even Nobody who ordered the fatal Balaklava cavalry charge. The non-relief of Kars was the work of Nobody, and Nobody has justly and severely suffered for that infamous transaction.

* * *

Surely, this is a rather wonderful state of things to be realising itself so long after the Flood, in such a country as England. Surely, it suggests to us with some force, that wherever this ubiquitous Nobody is, there mischief is and there danger is. For, it is especially to be borne in mind that wherever failure is accomplished, there Nobody lurks. With success, he has nothing to do. That is Everybody's business, and all manner of improbable people will invariably be found at the bottom of it. But, it is the great feature of the present epoch that all public disaster in the United Kingdom of Great Britain and Ireland is assuredly, and to a dead certainty, Nobody's work.

* * *

In civil matters we have Nobody equally active. When a civil office breaks down, the break-down is sure to be in Nobody's department. I entreat on my reader, dubious of this proposition, to wait until the next break-down (the reader is certain not to have to wait long), and to observe, whether or no, it is in Nobody's department. A dispatch of the greatest moment is sent to a minister abroad, at a most important crisis; Nobody reads it. British subjects are affronted in a foreign territory; Nobody interferes. Our own loyal fellow-subjects, a few thousand miles away, want to exchange political, commercial, and domestic intelligence with us; Nobody stops the mail. The government, with all its mighty means and appliances, is invariably beaten and outstripped by private enterprise; which we all know to be Nobody's fault. Something will be the national death of us, some day; and who can doubt that Nobody will be brought in Guilty?

From *Household Words*, 30 August 1856

WRITING

Could a similar article be written today? What would 'Nobody' be responsible for in *our* society? Try writing a present-day version of 'Nobody, Somebody and Everybody'.

FURTHER READING

Dickens also criticised the expensive and awkward process of patenting inventions in this country: you can read his article 'A Poor Man's Tale of a Patent' in *Reprinted Pieces*. This is also one of the themes of *Little Dorrit*, where Doyce, the inventor, is thwarted by officialdom. Read Chapter 10 for Doyce's account of his treatment by the Government.

FOR DISCUSSION

Do we still treat inventors and engineers badly? Are they better respected in other countries? How many of *you* are interested in engineering as a profession? What sort of image does it have?

Good ideas and practical projects

While Dickens was a powerful critic of his society there were many developments which he found exciting and hope-inspiring. In much of his journalism and speeches we find him enthusiastically supporting a wide range of institutions, inventions and practical projects.

The new police force, set up after the 1839 Royal Commission on Police, met with Dickens's approval.

THE DETECTIVE POLICE

We are not by any means devout believers in the old Bow Street Police. To say the truth, we think there was a vast amount of humbug about those worthies. Apart from many of them being men of very indifferent character, and far too much in the habit of consorting with thieves and the like, they never lost a public occasion of jobbing and trading in mystery and making the most of themselves. Continually puffed besides by incompetent magistrates anxious to conceal their own deficiencies, and hand-in-glove with the penny-a-liners of that time, they became a sort of superstition. Although as a Preventive Police they were utterly ineffective, and as a Detective Police were very loose and uncertain in their operations, they remain with some people a superstition to the present day.

On the other hand, the Detective Force organised since the establishment of the existing Police, is so well chosen and trained, proceeds so systematically and quietly, does its business in such a workmanlike manner, and is always so calmly and steadily engaged in the service of the public, that the public really do not know enough of it, to know a tithe of its usefulness. Impressed with this conviction, and interested in the men themselves, we represented to the authorities at Scotland Yard, that we should be glad, if there were no official objection, to have some talk with the Detectives. A most obliging and ready permission being given, a certain evening was appointed with a certain Inspector for a social conference between ourselves and the Detectives, at The Household Words Office in Wellington Street, Strand, London. In consequence of which appointment the party 'came off,' which we are about to describe. And we beg to repeat that, avoiding such topics as it might for obvious reasons be injurious to the public, or disagreeable to respectable individuals, to touch upon in print, our description is as exact as we can make it.

From 'The Detective Police' in *Reprinted Pieces*

The Hospital for Sick Children in London's Great Ormond Street, now one of the world's leading children's hospitals, received Dickens's support very early on in its history. It opened in 1852 and after six years was still a very small hospital and short of funds. Dickens spoke in its support at a charity dinner.

Now, ladies and gentlemen, such things need not be, and will not be, if this company, which is a drop of the life-blood of the great compassionate public heart, will only accept the means of rescue and prevention which is mine to offer. Within a quarter of a mile of this place where I speak, stands a courtly old house, where once, no doubt, blooming children were born, and grew up to be men and women, and married, and brought their own blooming children back to patter up the old oak staircase which stood but the other day, and to wonder at the old oak carvings on the chimney-pieces. In the airy wards into which the old state drawing-rooms and family bed-chambers of that house are now converted are such little patients that the attendant nurses look like reclaimed giantesses, and the kind medical practitioner like an amiable Christian ogre. Grouped about the little low tables in the centre of the rooms are such tiny convalescents that they seem to be playing at having been ill. On the dolls' beds are such diminutive creatures, that each poor sufferer is supplied with its tray of toys; and, looking around, you may see how the little tired, flushed cheek has toppled over half the brute creation on its way into the ark; or how one little dimpled arm has mowed down (as I saw myself) the whole tin soldiery of Europe. On the walls of these rooms are graceful, pleasant, bright, childish pictures. At the beds' heads, are pictures of the figure which is the universal embodiment of all mercy and compassion, the figure of Him who was once a child himself, and a poor one.

Besides these little creatures on the beds, you may learn in that place that the number of small Out-patients brought to that house for relief is no fewer than ten thousand in the compass of a single year. In the room in which these are received, you may see against the wall a box, on which it is written, that it has been calculated, that if every grateful mother who brings a child there will drop a penny into it, the Hospital funds may possibly be increased in a year by so large a sum as forty pounds. And you may read in the Hospital report, with a glow of pleasure, that these poor women are so respondent as to have made, even in a toiling year of difficulty and high prices, this estimated forty, fifty pounds. [*Cheers.*] In the printed papers of this same Hospital, you may read with what a generous earnestness the highest and wisest members of the medical profession testify to the great need of it; to the immense difficulty of treating children in the same hospitals with grown-up people, by reason of their different ailments and requirements; to the vast amount of pain that will be assuaged, and of the life that will be saved, through this Hospital – not only among the poor, observe, but among the prosperous too, by reason of the increased knowledge of children's illnesses, which cannot fail to arise from a more systematic mode of studying them. Lastly, gentlemen, and I am sorry to say, worst of all – (for I must present no rose-coloured picture of this place to you – I must not deceive you); lastly – the visitor to this Children's Hospital, reckoning up the number of its beds, will find himself perforce obliged to stop at very little over thirty; and will learn, with sorrow and surprise, that even that small number, so forlornly, so miserably diminutive, compared with this vast London, cannot possibly be maintained unless the Hospital be made better known; I limit myself to saying better known, because I will not believe that in a Christian community of fathers and mothers, and brothers and sisters, it can fail, being better known, to be well and richly endowed. [*Cheers.*]

From *Speech*, 9 February 1858

WRITING

Imagine you are a newspaper reporter present at this dinner. Write a brief summary of Dickens's speech for your newspaper.

Later that same year, Dickens made a speech in support of the provision of playgrounds for healthy children.

Some majestic minds out of doors may, for anything I know, and certainly for anything I care, consider it a very humdrum and low proceeding to stop, in a country full of steam-engines, power-looms, big ships, monster mortars, and great guns of all sorts, to consider where the children are to play. Nevertheless, I know that the question is a very kind one, and a very necessary one. [*Hear, hear.*] The surgeon and the recruiting sergeant will tell you with great emphasis, that the children's play is of immense importance to a community in the development of bodies; the clergyman, the schoolmaster, and the moral philosopher, in all degrees, will tell you with no less emphasis, that the children's play is of great importance to a community in the development of minds. I venture to assert that there can be no physical health without play; and there can be no efficient and satisfactory work without play; that there can be no sound and wholesome thought without play. [*Hear, hear.*] A country full of dismal little old men and women who had never played would be in a mighty bad way indeed; and you may depend upon it that without play, and good play, too, those powerful English cheers which have driven the sand of Asia before them, and made the very ocean shake, would degenerate into a puling whimper, that would be the most consolatory sound that can possibly be conceived to all the tyrants on the face of the earth.

Now, gentlemen, great towns constantly increasing about us, as the national trade and prosperity increase; houses constantly crowding together and continually accumulating; and the fields being always put at an always increasing distance from the great mass of the people; it becomes a very serious question where the children shall play, and how they shall grow up into men and women who must have played, or it would have been better for them and for all of us that they had never been born. The great importance of this question, in its many aspects both of humanity and policy, so strongly suggested itself to that gentleman who has been several times mentioned tonight – the Rev. Mr Laing – so strongly suggested itself to him, not yet a year ago, that he conceived the idea of establishing a Playground Society; in other words a combination of certain ladies and gentlemen of some influence and position who, being agreed on the main question, should resolve to advance it by all means in their power.

From *Speech*, 1 June 1858

FOR DISCUSSION

What arguments does Dickens put forward for the value of children's playgrounds?

FURTHER READING

Dickens was in favour of institutions that improved the quality of life for adults as well as children. See Chapter 4 of *The Uncommercial Traveller* for his piece about the Britannia Theatre, Hoxton, and Chapter 25 for another very positive piece about a self-supporting 'cooking depot' in London's East End.

He also took pleasure in some inventions and innovations: he was very pleased with the rail and ferry service that took him to Paris from London in eleven and a half hours – see 'A Flight', in *Reprinted Pieces* – and wrote with pleasure about a mechanical lathe that he saw at work in Chatham Dockyard – see *The Uncommercial Traveller*, Chapter 26.

Dickens not only appreciated other people's good ideas, but had a hand in a variety of projects himself. We have already seen how he involved himself with the Ragged Schools. At about the same time he also became involved with one of Dr Southwood Smith's projects. (We have come across Dr Southwood Smith in connection with the Public Health Movement.) The sanatorium was designed as a cheap hospital for lower-middle-class Londoners – for those often unmarried clerks and office juniors who lived in London alone and without the support of their families. If they fell ill there was often no one to look after them and Dr Southwood Smith realised that a subscription hospital could be set up to meet their needs. Dickens, who had lived and worked in London as a single young man, agreed that there was a need for such a hospital and gave it his vigorous support. It was opened in a house very near to Dickens's own house in Devonshire Terrace and Dickens spoke at its first anniversary festival.

Dickens was the guiding hand behind an institution designed for a very different type of clientele. During 1847 he started to advise Angela Burdett-Coutts on the setting-up of a home for the 'reclamation' of prostitutes. There were literally thousands of prostitutes in London, many of whom were frequently in prison for petty crime of one kind or another. (Prostitution itself was not a crime and neither was soliciting. Certain streets at certain times of the day became notorious for the number of prostitutes that were out and about.)

"*Familiar in their Mouths as* HOUSEHOLD WORDS."—SHAKESPEARE.

HOUSEHOLD WORDS.

A WEEKLY JOURNAL.

CONDUCTED BY CHARLES DICKENS.

Nº. 161.]

SATURDAY, APRIL 23, 1853.

[PRICE 2*d.*

HOME FOR HOMELESS WOMEN.

FIVE years and a half ago, certain ladies, grieved to think that numbers of their own sex were wandering about the streets in degradation, passing through and through the prisons all their lives, or hopelessly perishing in other ways, resolved to try the experiment on a limited scale of a Home for the reclamation and emigration of women. As it was clear to them that there could be little or no hope in this country for the greater part of those who might become the objects of their charity, they determined to receive into their Home, only those who distinctly accepted this condition: That they came there to be ultimately sent abroad, (whither, was at the discretion of the ladies); and that they also came there, to remain for such length of time as might, according to the circumstances of each individual case, be considered necessary as a term of probation, and for instruction in the means of obtaining an honest livelihood. The object of the Home was twofold. First, to replace young women who had already lost their characters and lapsed into guilt, in a situation of hope. Secondly, to save other young women who were in danger of falling into the like condition, and give them an opportunity of flying from crime when they and it stood face to face.

The projectors of this establishment, in undertaking it, were sustained by nothing but the high object of making some unhappy women a blessing to themselves and others instead of a curse, and raising up among the solitudes of a new world some virtuous homes, much needed there, from the sorrow and ruin of the old. They had no romantic visions or extravagant expectations. They were prepared for many failures and disappointments, and to consider their enterprise rewarded, if they in time succeeded with one third or one half of the cases they received.

As the experience of this small Institution, even under the many disadvantages of a beginning, may be useful and interesting, this paper will contain an exact account of its progress and results.

It was (and is) established in a detached house with a garden. The house was never designed for any such purpose, and is only adapted to it, in being retired **and** not immediately overlooked. It is capable of containing thirteen inmates besides two Superintendents. Excluding from consideration ten young women now in the house, there have been received in all, since November eighteen hundred and forty seven, fifty-six inmates. They have belonged to no particular class, but have been starving needlewomen of good character, poor needlewomen who have robbed their furnished lodgings, violent girls committed to prison for disturbances in ill-conducted workhouses, poor girls from Ragged Schools, destitute girls who have applied at Police offices for relief, young women from the streets: young women of the same class taken from the prisons after undergoing punishment there as disorderly characters, or for shoplifting, or for thefts from the person: domestic servants who have been seduced, and two young women held to bail for attempting suicide. No class has been favored more than another; and misfortune and distress are a sufficient introduction. It is not usual to receive women of more than five or six-and-twenty; the average age in the fifty-six cases would probably be about twenty. In some instances there have been great personal attractions; in others, the girls have been very homely and plain. The reception has been wholly irrespective of such sources of interest. Nearly all have been extremely ignorant.

Of these fifty-six cases, seven went away by their own desire during their probation; ten were sent away for misconduct in the Home; seven ran away; three emigrated and relapsed on the passage out; thirty (of whom seven are now married) on their arrival in Australia or elsewhere, entered into good service, acquired a good character, and have done so well ever since as to establish a strong prepossession in favor of others sent out from the same quarter. It will be seen from these figures that the failures are generally discovered in the Home itself, and that the amount of misconduct after the training and emigration, is remarkably small. And it is to be taken into consideration that many cases are admitted into the Home, of which there is, in the outset, very little hope, but which it is not deemed right to exclude from the experiment.

After a few years helping to run the Home anonymously, Dickens published a long article in *Household Words*, in which he described the work of the Home (see page 92). The article went on to give details of the rules and methods of running the Home.

As you can see from Dickens's account, not all the women were prostitutes, but most of them came to the home from prison.

(see page 92)

FOR DISCUSSION

1 Why do you think emigration was such an important part of the scheme?
2 What reasons might a woman have had for taking up a place in the Home?
3 Why do you think some of the inmates 'ran away'?

WRITING

Which modern institutions do you think Dickens would have supported? For example, what might he have written about a centre for the treatment of drug addicts? Try to write a piece in his style about such a modern institution.

One could argue that Dickens's most lasting institution was Christmas. It was Dickens who decided to celebrate Christmas with a special publication; the first being *A Christmas Carol*, published in 1843. He continued to write his Christmas books and stories for many years. He also, in his stories and in his personal life, placed great emphasis on the way Christmas, and the spirit of Christmas, brings people together, and makes them want to sink their differences rather than dwell on them. Dickens's writings about Christmas, particularly *A Christmas Carol*, have themselves become part of our idea of what Christmas is about. His description of the Cratchit family's Christmas dinner concentrates on the food and on the way the whole family is together and sharing their enjoyment.

Such a bustle ensued that you might have thought a goose the rarest of all birds; a feathered phenomenon, to which a black swan was a matter of course; and in truth it was something very like it in that house. Mrs Cratchit made the gravy (ready beforehand in a little saucepan) hissing hot; Master Peter mashed the potatoes with incredible vigour; Miss Belinda sweetened up the apple-sauce; Martha dusted the hot plates; Bob took Tiny Tim beside him in a tiny corner at the table; the two young Cratchits set chairs for everybody, not forgetting themselves, and mounting guard upon their posts, crammed spoons into their mouths, lest they should shriek for goose before their turn came to be helped. At last the dishes were set on, and grace was said. It was succeeded by a breathless pause, as Mrs Cratchit, looking slowly all along the carving-knife, prepared to plunge it in the breast; but when she did, and when the long expected gush of stuffing issued forth, one murmur of delight arose all round the board, and even Tiny Tim, excited by the two young Cratchits, beat on the table with the handle of his knife, and feebly cried Hurrah!

There never was such a goose. Bob said he didn't believe there ever was such a goose cooked. Its tenderness and flavour, size and cheapness, were the themes of universal admiration. Eked out by the apple-sauce and mashed potatoes, it was a sufficient dinner for the whole family; indeed, as Mrs Cratchit said with great delight (surveying one small atom of a bone upon the dish), they hadn't ate it all at last! Yet every one had had enough, and the youngest Cratchits in particular, were steeped in sage and onion to the eyebrows! But now, the plates being changed by Miss Belinda, Mrs Cratchit left the room alone – too nervous to bear witnesses – to take the pudding up, and bring it in.

Suppose it should not be done enough! Suppose it should break in turning out! Suppose somebody should have got over the wall of the back-yard, and stolen it, while they were merry with the goose: a supposition at which the two young Cratchits became livid! All sorts of horrors were supposed.

Hallo! A great deal of steam! The pudding was out of the copper. A smell like a washing-day! That was the cloth. A smell like an eating-house, and a pastry cook's next door to each other, with a laundress's next door to that! That was the pudding. In half a minute Mrs Cratchit entered: flushed, but smiling proudly: with the pudding, like a speckled cannon-ball, so hard and firm, blazing in half of half-a-quartern of ignited brandy, and bedight with Christmas holly stuck into the top.

Oh, a wonderful pudding! Bob Cratchit said, and calmly too, that he regarded it as the greatest success achieved by Mrs Cratchit since their marriage. Mrs Cratchit said that now the weight was off her mind, she would confess she had had her doubts about the quantity of flour. Everybody had something to say about it, but nobody said or thought it was at all a small pudding for a large family. It would have been flat heresy to do so. Any Cratchit would have blushed to hint at such a thing.

At last the dinner was all done, the cloth was cleared, the hearth swept, and the fire made up. The compound in the jug being tasted, and considered perfect, apples and oranges were put upon the table, and a shovel-full of chestnuts on the fire. Then all the Cratchit family drew round the hearth, in what Bob Cratchit called a circle, meaning half a one; and at Bob Cratchit's elbow stood the family display of glass; two tumblers and a custard-cup without a handle.

These held the hot stuff from the jug, however, as well as golden goblets would have done; and Bob served it out with beaming looks, while the chestnuts on the fire sputtered and crackled noisily. Then Bob proposed:

'A Merry Christmas to us all, my dears. God bless us!'

Which all the family re-echoed.

'God bless us every one!' said Tiny Tim, the last of all.

From *A Chrismas Carol*, Stave 3, pp. 95–7

Dickens did not invent Christmas the religious festival, but we could say he invented Christmas the institution!

We have seen in this chapter how Dickens was involved with a wide range of ideas and institutions during his lifetime. His setting up of his own journal in 1850 gave him a powerful means of broadcasting his opinions and, as we have seen, he was not shy about doing so. He built his reputation as a novelist, but his influence as a public figure was spread through his work as a journalist, editor and, according to some, the most brilliant after-dinner speaker of his time.

Select bibliography

DICKENS'S LIFE AND LETTERS

Chistopher Hibbert's *The Making of Charles Dickens* (1967) is now published in paperback (Penguin, 1983) and is the best short biography available.

The most recent biography is *Dickens: A Life*, by N. and J. MacKenzie (Oxford University Press, 1979). Another modern biography is Edgar Johnson's *Charles Dickens: His Tragedy and Triumph* (1977), available in paperback and well indexed (Penguin 1986).

John Forster's *Life of Charles Dickens* is available in a modern, two-volume edition and includes a great deal of documentary material (Dent Everyman's Library, 1970).

Interesting biographical material is collected in *Dickens: Interviews and Recollections*, edited by Philip Collins in two volumes (Macmillan, 1981).

A very useful, single-volume selection of the letters, *Selected Letters of Charles Dickens*, edited by David Paroissien, is available in paperback (Macmillan, 1985).

NOVELS

The best paperback edition is the Oxford World Classics, but it is not yet a complete series. However, Penguin publishes all the novels in good, reliable editions.

JOURNALISM AND TRAVEL WRITING

The two travel books – *American Notes* and *Pictures from Italy* – and the two books of journalism – *Reprinted Pieces* and *The Uncommercial Traveller* – are all published by Oxford University Press. A collection of journalism on social issues has now been published under the title *A December Vision*, edited by Neil Philip and Victor Neuberg (Collins, 1986).

SPEECHES AND READINGS

Collected Speeches, edited by K. J. Fielding (Oxford University Press, 1960), is the standard edition of the speeches. The public readings have been collected together and edited by Philip Collins – *Charles Dickens: Public Readings* (Oxford University Press, 1975). These have been reprinted in paperback – *Sikes and Nancy and Other Public Readings* (Oxford University Press, 1983).

Index of extracts